# Latin American Society and Legal Culture

**Recent Titles in**
**Bibliographies and Indexes in Law and Political Science**

Scottish Nationalism and Cultural Identity in the Twentieth Century: An Annotated Bibliography of Secondary Sources
*Compiled by Gordon Bryan*

Edwin S. Corwin and the American Constitution:
A Bibliographical Analysis
*Kenneth D. Crews*

Political Risk Assessment: An Annotated Bibliography
*Compiled by David A. Jodice*

Human Rights: An International and Comparative Law Bibliography
*Compiled and Edited by Julian R. Friedman and Marc I. Sherman*

# Latin American Society and Legal Culture

## A BIBLIOGRAPHY

Compiled by Frederick E. Snyder

Bibliographies and Indexes in Law and Political Science, Number 5

Greenwood Press
Westport, Connecticut • London, England

**Library of Congress Cataloging in Publication Data**

Snyder, Frederick E.
Latin American society and legal culture.

(Bibliographies and indexes in law and political science, ISSN 0742-6909 ; no. 5)
Includes index.
1. Law—Latin America—Bibliography. 2. Latin America—Politics and government—1948- —Bibliography.
I. Title. II. Series.
KG1.S68 1985 016.3498 85-5593
016.348
ISBN 0-313-24858-3 (lib. bdg. : alk. paper)



Library of Congress Catalog Card Number: 85-5593
ISBN: 0-313-24858-3
ISSN: 0742-6909

First published in 1985

Greenwood Press
A division of Congressional Information Service, Inc.
88 Post Road West
Westport, Connecticut 06881

Printed in the United States of America

The paper used in this book complies with the Permanent Paper Standard issued by the National Information Standards Organization (Z39.48-1984).

10 9 8 7 6 5 4 3 2 1

# CONTENTS

# *INTRODUCTION*

Developed in tandem with my own efforts to design a course at Harvard Law School, this bibliography presents and explains the distinctive attitudes toward law, legal institutions and processes that have emerged from the tumultuous histories of Mexico, Cuba, Nicaragua, Peru, Chile, Colombia, Venezuela, Argentina, Brazil and the other Latin American societies. Over 2,000 references to materials collectively provide useful insight into the Latin American legal experience as a whole.

Throughout the past thirty or forty years, legal scholars in the United States have pursued a number of varying approaches to the study of Latin American law, politics and society. For example, the "place" of the Latin American phenomenon within the legal systems of the Western Hemisphere provided the framework for Henry P. deVries' pioneering course at Columbia University School of Law.[1] Kenneth Karst and Keith S. Rosenn focused on the legal dimensions that Latin Americans have had to face as members of societies undergoing the process of economic development.[2]

---

1. His material has been compiled in Henry P. deVries, Cases and Materials on the Law of the Americas: An Outline of Latin American Law and Society. New York: Parker School of Foreign and Comparative Law, Columbia University (1980).

2. Kenneth Karst and Keith S. Rosenn, Law and Development in Latin America: A Casebook. Berkeley: University of California Press (1975).

John H. Merryman and David S. Clark described Latin American legal experiences primarily as variations on the Civil Law tradition inherited from Western Europe.[3] More recently, Albert S. Golbert and Yenny Nun highlighted major developments in certain fundamental substantive areas of the law (constitutional, property, contracts, corporations, trade regulation, labor, international) that have affected the legal systems of many large Latin American countries.[4] In addition to these approaches, other treatments of Latin American legal systems, both general and specific by country, are cited in a guide to basic research in Latin American legal studies that I have recently published.[5]

This bibliography fulfills a different need. I wanted to identify the available material that would illuminate how economic, political and social developments in Latin America affected perceptions, refinements and uses of those constructs and commentaries we characterize as legal (i.e., laws, legal ideas, institutions and processes). The course I ultimately developed and taught for the past three years, Law, Politics and Revolution in Latin America, addressed these issues in the same order as the outline of this Bibliography.

---

3. John H. Merryman and David S. Clark, Comparative Law: Western European and Latin American Legal Systems. Indianapolis: Bobbs-Merrill (1978).

4. Albert S. Golbert and Yenny Nun, Latin American Laws and Institutions. New York: Praeger (1982).

5. Frederick E. Snyder, Latin American Legal Studies: A Guide to Basic Research. Cambridge, Massachusetts: Harvard Law School (1984).

While preparing this course, I found that none of the available bibliographies of Latin America fully suited my very particular purposes.[6] Such major compilations of Latin American culture (literature, political science, history, sociology, economics) as the Bibliographic Guide to Latin American Studies[7] contained relatively few citations to primary or secondary legal literature, though enormously rich in contextual references. Not unexpectedly, legal bibliographies[8] presented the opposite disadvantage: Usually organized in a highly formal way with citations to recent books and articles, these bibliographies explored developments in the purely doctrinal areas of domestic and international law. From my initial explorations, then, I sensed a serious need for a bibliography citing the major themes of legal life in Latin America within the broader context of the economic, political, social and historic currents, lending greater substance to those particular themes. The reading list compiled here satisfies that need.

---

6. Citations to all major bibliographies of Latin American material, legal and non-legal, are contained in my research guide. See note 5.

7. Bibliographic Guide to Latin American Studies. Boston: G.K. Hall (1984).

8. Such as Richard J. Navarro, A Bibliography of Latin American Law: Primary and Secondary materials in English. 19 Tex. Int'l L.J. 319 (1984); Charles A. Sladitz, Bibliography on Foreign and Comparative Law, Books and Articles in English. Dobbs Ferry: Oceana Publications (editions in 1955, 1962, 1968, 1975 and 1980). For a more contextual approach, see S.A. Bayitch, Latin-America: A Bibliographical Guide to Economy, History, Law, Politics, and Society. Coral Gables: Interamerican Legal Studies (1961). This edition, however, is largely out of date today.

Part One, "Pressures of History and Tradition on the Law, Legal Institutions and Processes of Latin America," includes references to primary and secondary sources, depicting most of what is known about the background and character of legal life in Latin America before the discoveries by European explorers and during the period of Iberian colonial rule. Most of this literature is in Spanish and Portuguese and remains as yet untranslated into English.

Part Two, "Varieties of Legal Experience in Latin America: The Interplay of Politics, Economics, Ideology and Convention," contains the following references to representative and interpretive material in English, Spanish and Portuguese: major movements in Latin American jurisprudence and their relationship to general intellectual developments; analyses and commentaries on the interactions between political, military, and social history of Latin America; movements to codify the law; and Latin American constitutionalism. In addition, this section includes texts describing and explicating the more procedural elements of Latin American legal culture, such as the education of future law-makers, the organization of the legal profession, and the process of justice. This part does not cite such relevant primary material as the various codes, constitutions, and cases that have surfaced throughout the history of the different Latin American republics; information regarding access to this voluminous material is available, however, in my research guide[9] and, more summarily, through the International Encyclopedia of Comparative Law.[10]

Part Three, "Dreams of Vindication: Revolutionary and Other Responses to the Ravages of Dependency and the Challenges of Development," addresses the different strategies that substantive law has followed in response to the crucial political and economic crises of Latin America in the modern history. The readings here describe and elucidate the efforts, through various legal modalities, of corporatist, authoritarian, and revolutionary socialist governments to come to grips with the often conflicting demands in their societies for economic development, enhanced State power and personal freedom, all in the face of national and regional dependence on the financial and geopolitical power of the industrialized First World nations. The part explores these themes in connection with the following areas of substantive law: land reform; housing and urban law; commercial law; corporation law; labor law; consumer and environmental law; welfare law; income taxation; estates and trusts; civil rights of women, children, minorities and indigenous populations; regulation of foreign investment; international law; human rights; and regional economic integration law.

As a whole, this bibliography is designed as a guide primarily for lawyers, legal scholars and social scientists

---

9. See note 5.

10. Victor Knapp, ed., International Encyclopedia of Comparative Law. Tubingen: J.C.B. MOHR (1972).

in need of an introduction to the basic and current material on the relationships between law, society, economics and politics in Latin America. The work consists of citations to books, articles, magazine and newspaper reports, monographs and doctoral dissertations produced up to November 1, 1984. Most of the citations refer to works written in English, assuming that such will be the primary language of the readers; but my goal has also been to include references to the important works in Spanish and Portuguese (untranslated) as well. I have omitted citations to material not generally available in the United States. Much of my research was conducted at the Library of Congress, Widener Library of Harvard University, and the International Legal Studies Library of Harvard Law School.

My hope is that this bibliography will make some contribution to the study of the legal cultures of Latin America on their own terms. Personal freedom, social and economic justice, the accumulation and regulation of state power--all modern societies have had to manage the tensions underlying these elusive aspirations, and many in doing so have fashioned legal experiences rich in imagery and both positive and negative in example. The legal life of Latin America has its part to play in this study as well.

## *ABBREVIATIONS*

| | |
|---|---|
| CEDES | Centro de Estudios de Estado y Sociedad (Argentina) |
| CEDYS | Centro de Estudios de Derecho y Sociedad (Peru) |
| HAHR | Hispanic American Historical Review |
| ISHI | Institute for the Study of Human Issues |
| SAIS | School of Advanced International Studies (Johns Hopkins University) |
| UNAM | Universidad Nacional Autonoma de Mexico |

Note: For law review publications, consult A Uniform System of Citation, 13th edition (1981), published by Harvard Law Review Association, Harvard Law School, Cambridge, Massachusetts.

# Latin American Society and Legal Culture

# *I. PRESSURES OF HISTORY AND TRADITION ON THE LAW, LEGAL INSTITUTIONS AND PROCESSES OF LATIN AMERICA*

## A. Pre-Colombian Ghost Stories: Indian Icons in Modern Latin American Legal Culture


1. Adams, Richard E. Prehistoric Mesoamerica. Boston: Little Brown (1977).

2. Alba, Hermosillo Carlos. Estudio comparado entre el Derecho Azteca y el Derecho positivo Mexicano. México: Edición Especial del Instituto Indigenista Interamericano (1949).

3. Avila, P. Francisco de. Narratives of the Rites and Laws of the Incas. Trans. C.R. Markham. 48 Hakl. Soc., 1st Ser. 121 (1873).

4. Bandelier, Adolph R. On the Distribution and Tenure of Lands, and the Customs with Respect to Inheritance, among the Ancient Mexicans. Eleventh Annual Report of the Peabody Museum of American Archaeology and Ethnology. Salem: Salem Press (1878).

5. Baudin, Louis. A Socialist Empire: The Incas of Peru. trans. Katherine Woods. Princeton: Van Nostrand (1961).

6. Bernal, Ignacio. The Olmec World. Trans. Doris Heyden & Fernando Horcasitas. Berkeley: Univ. of Cal. Press (1969).

7. Bingham, Hiram. Lost City of the Incas: The Story of Machu Picchu and Its Builders. Westport, Conn: Greenwood Press (1981).

8. Boban, Eugene. Documents pour servir à l'histoire du Mexique. 2 vols. Paris: E. Leroux (1891).

9. The Book of Chilam Balam of Chumayel. G.B. Gordon, ed. Philadelphia: University Museum (1913).

10. Brinton, Daniel G. The Maya Chronicles. Philadelphia: Library of Aboriginal American Literature Vol 1. Philadelphia: D.G. Brinton (1882).

11. Brotherston, Gordon. Image of the New World: The American Continent Portrayed in Native Texts London: Thames & Hudson (1979).

12. Burns, E. Bradford. Latin America: A Concise Interpretive History. 3rd ed. Englewood Cliffs: Prentice Hall (1982).

13. Carrera-Stampa, Manuel. Fuentes para el Estudio de la Historia Indígena. 2 Esplendor del Mexico Antiguo 1109 (1959).

14. Casas, Bartolomé de las. The Horrors of the Conque[st] in Bartolomé de las Casas: A Selection of His Writings. Trans. and ed. George Sanderlin. New York: Knopf (1971).

15. Caso, Alfonso. The Aztecs: People of the Sun, Norman: Univ. of Oklahoma Press (1958).

16. Chagnon, Napoleon A. Yanomamo: The Fierce People, 2d ed. New York: Holt Rinehart (1977).

17. Chamberlain, Robert S. Simpson's The Encomienda in New Spain and Recent Encomienda Studies. 34 HAHR 238 (1954).

18. Cieza de León, Pedro de. The War of Quito and Inca Documents. Trans. and ed. Clements R. Markham London: Hakluyt Society (1913).

19. Cobo, El Padre Bernabé. Historia del Nuevo Mundo. Ed. Jimenez de la Espada. Sevilla (1890-93).

20. Codex Mendoza. Ed. & trans., James Cooper Clark. 3 vols. London: Waterlow & Sons (1938).

21. Códice Pérez. Ed. & Trans., Emile Solís Alcalá. Mérida, Yucatán: Liga de Acción Social (1949).

22. Coe, M.D. The Maya. New York: Praeger (1966).

23. Comas, Juan. Ensayos sobre indigenismo. México: Instituto Indigenista Inter-Americano (1953).

24. Cortés, Hernán. Cartas de relación de la conquista de Mexico. Mexico City: Editorial Porrúa (1961).

25. Davies, Nigel. The Aztecs. Norman: Univ. of Oklahoma Press (1980).

26. Díaz del Castillo, Bernal. The Conquest of New Spain. Trans. J.M. Cohen. New York: Penguin Books (1963).

27. Dibble, C.E., ed. Historia de la nación Mexicana; Reproducción a todo color del Códice de 1576 (Códice Aubin). Madrid: J. Porrúa Turanzas (1963).

28. Edmonson, Munro S. The Chilam Balam of Tizimin. Austin: Univ. of Texas Press (1982).

29. ____________________, trans. and ed. The Popol Vuh: The Quiche Book of Counsel. New Orleans: Middle American Research Institute, Tulane University (1971).

30. Eguiguren, Luis A. El ayullu peruano y su condición legal. Lima (1914).

31. Florentine Codex: General History of the Things of New Spain. Trans. (from the Aztec) by C. Dibble and A.J.O. Anderson. 12 vols. Santa Fe: Univ. of New Mexico Press (1950-1975).

32. Frau, Salvador. Las Civilizaciones Prehispánicas de América. Buenos Aires: Editorial Sudamericana (1955).

33. Fried, Jacob. The Relation of Ideal Norms to Actual Behavior in Tarahumara Society. 9 Southwestern Journal of Anthropology 286 (Autumn, 1953).

34. Gibson, Charles. The Aztecs under Spanish Rule. Stanford: Stanford Univ. Press (1964).

35. ____________________. The Inca Concept of Sovereignty and the Spanish Administration of Peru. Austin: University of Texas Latin American Studies (1948).

36. Gillin, John. The Making of a Witch Doctor. 19 Psychiatry 131 (May, 1956).

37. _________________. Magical Fright. 11 Psychiatry 387 (November, 1948).

38 Góngora, Mario. El Estado en el Derecho Indiano, época de fundación, 1492-1570. Santiago de Chile: Instituto de Investigaciones Historico-Culturales, Facultad de Filosofía y Educación, Univ. de Chile (1951).

39. Grieder, Terence. Demons and Discipline in Ancient Peru. 67 Art News (Oct. 1968).

40. Handbook of Middle American Indians. Robert Wauchope, gen. ed. Austin: Univ. of Texas Press (1964-1975).

41. Handbook of South American Indians. Julian Steward, ed. Washington: Smithsonian (1944-1959).

42. Hanke, Lewis. The Spanish Struggle for Justice in the Conquest of America. Boston: Little Brown (1965).

43. ______________. Aristotle and the American Indians. London: Hollis & Carter (1959).

44. Hemming, John. The Conquest of the Incas. New York: Harcourt Brace (1970).

45. Humphreys, R.A. Economic Aspects of the Fall of the Spanish American Empire. 30 Revista de historia de America, 450 (December, 1950).

46. Keen, Benjamin. The Aztec Image in Western Thought. New Brunswick: Rutgers Univ. Press (1971).

47. Kirchhoff, Paul. Land Tenure in Ancient Mexico. 14 Revista Mexicana de Estudios Antropológicos 251, Part 1 (1954-55).

48. Kohler, J. El Derecho de los Aztecas. México: Revista Jurídica de la Escuela Libre de Derecho (1924).

49. Krickeberg, Walter. Altmexikanische Kulturen. Berlin: Safari-Verlag (1956).

50. La Faye, Jacques. Quetzalcoatl and Guadalupe. Chicago: Univ. of Chicago Press (1976).

51. Landa, Fray Diego de. Yucatán. Trans. William Gates. New York: Dover Publications (1978).

52. León-Portilla, Miguel. Aztec Thought and Culture: A Study of the Ancient Nahuatl Mind. Trans. J.E. Davis. Norman: Univ. of Oklahoma Press (1963).

53. ____________________. The Broken Spears. The Aztec Account of the Conquest. Trans. Lysander Kemp. Boston: Beacon Press (1962).

54. León-Portilla, Miguel and Salvador Mateos Higuera. Catálogo de los Códices Indigenas del México Antiguo. Suplemento del Boletín Bibliográfico de la Secretaría de Hacienda, Año 3, No. 111. México (1957).

55. Lockhart, James. Spanish Peru 1532-1560. Madison: Univ. of Wisconsin Press (1968).

56. Lovenson, Brian. Chile - The Legacy of Hispanic Capitalism. New York: Oxford Univ. Press (1979).

57. Lumbreras, Luis G. The Peoples And Cultures of Ancient Peru. Trans. Betty J. Meggers. Washington: Smithsonian (1974).

58. Lynch, John. Spanish Colonial Administration, 1782-1810: The Intendant System in the Viceroyalty of Rio de la Plata. Univ. of London Historical Studies, 5. London: Athlone Press (1958).

59. MacLachlan, C. Criminal Justice in Eighteenth Century Mexico. Berkeley: Univ. of Cal. Press (1974).

60. Mariátegui, José Carlos. Seven Interpretive Essays on Peruvian Reality. Trans. Marjory Uquidi. Austin: Univ. of Texas Press (1971).

61. Martin, Luis. The Kingdom of the Sun: A Short History of Peru. New York: Scribner (1974).

62. Mason, J. Alden. The Ancient Civilizations of Peru. Rev. ed. Harmondsworth, Eng.: Penguin (1975).

63. Means, Philip A. Indian Legislation in Peru. 3 Hispanic Amer. Hist. Rev. 509 (1920).

64. ________________. Fall of the Inca Empire and the Spanish Rule in Peru, 1530-1780. New York: Gordian Press (1964).

65. Molina, Cristóbal de. The Narratives of the Rites and Laws of the Incas. Trans. C.R. Markham. London: Hakluyt Society (1873).

66. Molina Enríquez, Andrés. Los grandes problemas nacionales. Mexico: Era (1979).

67. Moore, Sally Falk. Power and Property in Inca Peru. New York: Columbia Univ. Press (1958).

68. Morley, Sylvanus. The Ancient Maya. 3d ed. Stanford: Stanford Univ. Press (1956).

69. Murra, J.V. La organización económica del Estado Inca. México: Siglo xxi (1978).

70. Nichols, Madaline W. Las Siete Partidas. 20 Cal. L. Rev. 260 (1932).

71. Offner, Jerome A. Law and Politics in Aztec Texcoco. New York: Cambridge Univ. Press (1983).

72. OtsCapdequí, José M. Historia del Derecho Español en América y del Derecho Indiano. Madrid: Aguilar (1968).

73. Parry, John H. The Spanish Seaborne Empire. London: Hutchinson (1966).

74. Paz, Octavio. The Other Mexico: Critique of the Pyramid. Trans. Lysander Kemp. New York: Grove Press (1972).

75. Pendle, George. A History of Latin America. Middlesex: Penguin Books (1980).

76. Phelan, John Leddy. The Kingdom of Quito in the Seventeenth Century: Bureaucratic Politics in the Spanish Empire. Madison: Univ. of Wisconsin Press (1967).

77. Picón-Salas, Mariano. A Cultural History of Spanish America: From Conquest to Independence. Berkeley: Univ. of California Press (1962).

78. Polo de Ondegardo, Juan. Of the Lineage of the Incas and How They Extended Their Conquests in Rites and Laws of the Incas. Trans. Clements R. Markham. London: Hakluyt Society (1873).

79. Prado, Caio. The Colonial Background of Modern Brazil. Trans. Suzette Macedo. Berkeley: Univ. of Cal. Press (1967).

80. Prescott, William H. History of the Conquest of Mexico. Rev. ed., 3 vols. Philadelphia: J. P. Lippincott (1874).

81. ____________________. History of the Conquest of Peru. New York: Harper & Bros. (1847).

82. Rosenblat, Angel. La población de America en 1492. Viejos y nuevos cálculos. Mexico: El Colegio de Mexico (1967).

83. ________________. La población indígena y el mestizaje en America. Buenos Aires: Ed. Nova (1954).

84. Rowe, John H. "Inca Culture at the Time of the Spanish Conquest," in Handbook of South American Indians. Ed. Julian H. Steward. Vol. II. Washington: U.S. Gov't. Printing Off. (1946).

85. ________________. The Incas under Spanish Colonial Institutions. 32 Hispanic American Hist. Rev. 155-199 (1957).

86. Sahagun, Bernardino de. Codex Florentino: Illustrations for Sahagun's Historia General de las Cosas de Nueva España. Francisco del Paso y Troncoso, ed. Vol. 5 Madrid (1905).

87. __________. Florentine Codex: General History of the Things of New Spain. Trans. Arthur J. O. Anderson and Charles E. Dibble. Santa Fe: Univ. of Utah and School of American Research (1975).

88. Scott, G., ed. Las Siete Partidas. Chicago: Commerce Clearing House (1931).

89. Sejourné, Laurette. Burning Water: Thought and Religion in Ancient Mexico. Berkeley: Shamhala (1976).

90. Sheridan, Thomas E. and Thomas H. Naylor, eds. Raramuri: A Tarahumara Colonial Chronicle 1607-1791. Flagstaff, Arizona: Northland Press (1979).

91. Soustelle, Jacques. Daily Life of the Aztecs on the Eve of the Spanish Conquest. Trans. Patrick O'Brian. Stanford: Stanford Univ. Press (1961).

92. Stein, Stanley & Barbara H. Stein. The Colonial Heritage of Latin America: Essays on Economic Dependence in Perspective. New York: Oxford Univ. Press (1970).

93. Sten, María. Las extraordinarias historias de los Códices Mexicanos. Mexico City: J. Moritz (1972).

94. Tax, Sol. The Civilizations of Ancient America. Chicago: Univ. of Chicago Press (1951).

95. Thompson, J. Eric. Maya History and Religion. Norman: Univ. of Oklahoma Press (1970).

96. Trimborn, Hermann. Straftat und Sühne in Alt Peru. 57 Zeitschrift für Ethnologie 194 (1925).

97. Urteaga, Horacio H. El imperio incaico. En el que se incluye la historia del ayllo y familia de los Incas. Lima: Librería e Imprenta Gil (S.A.)(1931).

98. ______________. La organización judicial en el imperio de los Incas. 9 Revista histórica 1 Lima: Libreria e Imprenta Gil (S.A.) 1928).

99. Vaillant, George C. Aztecs of Mexico. 2nd ed. New York: Penguin Books (1962).

100. Valencia, Matus. The Centenary of the Chilean Civil Code. 7 Am. J. Comp. L. 71 (1958).

101. Garcilaso de la Vega. The Incas. Trans. María Jolas, ed. Alain Gheerbrant. New York: Orion Press (1961).

102. Von Hagen, Victor W. The Realm of the Incas. New York: New American Library (1957).

103. Wachtel, Nathan. The Vision of the Vanquished: The Spanish Conquest of Peru through Indian Eyes, 1530-1570. New York: Barnes and Noble (1977).

104. Wauchope, Robert, ed. The Indian Background of Latin American History: The Maya, Aztec, Inca and Their Predecessors. New York: Knopf (1970).

105. Whitaker, Arthur P., ed. Latin America and the Enlightenment. Ithaca, N.Y.: Great Seal Books (1961).

106. Wicke, Charles. Olmec. Tucson: Univ. of Arizona Press (1971).

107. Wolf, Eric. Sons of the Shaking Earth. Chicago: Univ. of Chicago Press (1959).

108. Woodward, Ralph Lee, Jr. Central America: A Nation Divided. New York: Oxford Univ. Press (1976).

109. Xerez, Francisco de. Reports on the Discovery of Peru. Trans. C.R. Markham. Hakluyt Society, 1st ser., 47, 1-109 (1872).

110. Zavala, Silvio. El mundo americano en la época colonial. México: Editoria Porrúa (1967).

111. __________. The Political Philosophy of the Conquest of America. Mexico: Editorial Cultura (1953).

112. Zorita, Alonso de. Life and Labor in Ancient Mexico. Trans. Benjamin Keen. New Brunswick: Rutgers Univ. Press (1963).

B. Conquistadores, Caudillos, Catholicism: The Resonance of the Colonial Experience in Modern Latin American Legal Culture.

113. Alden, Dauril. Royal Government in Colonial Brazil. Berkeley: Univ. of Cal. Press (1968).

114. Altamira, Rafael. El Texto de las Leyes de Burgos de 1512. 4 Revista de historia de America 5 (1938).

115. Alvarez, Jose María. Las instituciones de derecho real de Castilla y de Indias. Mexico: UNAM (1982).

116. Anderson, Arthur J.O., Frances Berdan and James Lockhart, eds. Beyond the Codices: The Nahua View of Colonial Mexico. Berkeley: Univ. of Cal. Press (1976).

117. Beezley, W.H. Caudillismo: An Interpretive Note. 11 J. Inter-Am. Stud. (July 1969).

118. Beleña, Eusebio B. Recopilación sumaria de todos los autos acordados de la Real Audiencia y Sala del Crimen de esta Nueva España. México: UNAM (1981).

119. Benson, Nettie Lee, ed. Mexico and the Spanish Cortes, 1910-1822; Eight Essays. Austin, Texas: Univ. of Texas Press for the Institute of Latin American Studies (1966).

120. Blanksten, George I. Ecuador: Constitutions Caudillos. New York: Russell & Russell (1964).

121. Borah, Woodrow. Justice by Insurance: The General Indian Court of Colonial Mexico and the Legal Aides of the Half-Real. Berkeley: Univ. of California Press (1983).

122. Boxer, C.R. The Golden Age of Brazil 1695-1750. Berkeley: Univ. of Cal. Press (1962).

123. Browning, David S. Historic Basis of Mexican Mining Laws. 7 Inter-Am. L. Rev. 1 (1965).

124. Burkholder, Mark A. Politics of a Colonial Career: Jose Baquijano and the Audiencia of Lima. Albuquerque: Univ. of New Mexico Press (1980).

125. Burns, E. Bradford. *Latin America: A Concise Interpretive History*. 3rd ed. Englewood Cliffs: Prentice Hall (1982).

126. Campbell, E. Church and State in Colonial Peru: The Bishop of Cuzco and the Tupac Amaru Rebellion of 1780. 22 *J. Church and State* 251 (1980).

127. Carter, Constance A. Law and Society in Colonial Mexico. Ph.D. Thesis, Columbia University (1971).

128. Castañeda, Carlos E. The Corregidor in Spanish Colonial Administration. 9 *HAHR* 130 (1929).

129. Castro, Américo. *The Structure of Spanish History*. Trans. E.L. King Princeton: Princeton U. Press (1954).

130. Chalmers, D.A. Colonial Institutions and Contemporary Latin America. 43 *HAHR* I (August 1963).

131. Chamberlain, Robert S. The Concept of the Señor Natural as Revealed by Castilian Law and Administration Documents. 19 *HAHR* 130 (1939).

132. ______________________. Simpson's The Encomienda in New Spain and Recent Encomienda Studies. 34 *HAHR* 238 (1954).

133. ______________________. "Castilian Backgrounds of the Repartamiento-Encomienda," in Carnegie Institution, 5 *Contributions to American Anthropology and History* 21 (no. 25) (1939).

134. Chance, John K. *Race and Class in Colonial Oaxaca*. Stanford: Stanford Univ. Press (1978).

135. Chevalier, Francois. *Land and Society in Colonial Mexico. The Great Hacienda*. Berkeley: Univ. of California Press (1963).

136. Clark, David S. Judicial Protection of the Constitution in Latin America. 2 *Hast. Con. L. Q*. 405 (1975).

137. Clark, James Cooper, trans. & ed. *Codex Mendoza*. London: Waterlow & Sons (1938).

138. Cortes, Hernando. *Letters from Mexico*. Trans. & ed. A.R. Padgen. New York: Grossman (1971).

139. Coy, P.E.B. Justice for the Indian in Eighteenth Century Mexico. 12 *Am. J. Legal Hist*. 41 (1968).

140. Cunha, Euclydes da. Rebellion in the Backlands. Trans. Samuel Putnam, Chicago: Univ. of Chicago Press (1970).

141. Dart, Henry P. The Influence of the Ancient Laws of Spain on the Jurisprudence of Louisiana. 1 Inter-Am. L. Rev. 303 (1959).

142.. Davidson, Theresa S. "The Brazilian Inheritance of Roman Law," in Watson, J., ed. Four Papers Presented in the Institute of Brazilian Studies Vanderbilt University. Nashville: Vanderbilt Univ. Press (1953).

143. Dealy, Glen. Prolegomena on the Spanish American Political Tradition. 48 HAHR 37 (1968).

144. Díaz del Castillo, Bernal. The Discovery and Conquest of Mexico. Trans. A.P. Maudslay. New York: Farrar Straus & Cudahy (1956).

145. Domínguez, Jorge. Insurrection or Loyalty: the Breakdown of the Spanish American Empire. Cambridge: Harvard Univ. Press (1980).

146. Enzinas, Diego de. Cedulario indiano. Madrid: Ediciones Cultura Hispánica (1945-46).

147. __________________. Recopilacion de leyes de los reynos de las Indias. 4 vols. Madrid (1681).

148. Fisher, Lillian Estelle. Viceregal Administration in the Spanish American Colonies. Berkeley: Univ. of Cal. Press (1926).

149. Gibson, Charles. Spain in America. New York: Harper-Row (1966).

150. __________________. The Spanish Tradition in America. Columbia: Univ. of So. Car. Press (1968).

151. __________________. The Inca Concept of Sovreignty and the Spanish Administration of Peru. Austin: Univ. of Texas Press (1948).

152. __________________. The Aztecs Under Spanish Rule. Stanford: Stanford Univ. Press (1964).

153. González, María del Refugio. Historia del Derecho Mexicano. México: UNAM (1981).

154. Graham, Richard. Independence in Latin America. New York: Knopf (1972).

155. Griffin, Charles C. Economic and Social Aspects of the Era of Spanish-American Independence. 22 HAHR 170 (1949).

156. Hakluyt, Richard. "The Voyage of Miles Philips," in The Principal Navigations, Voyages, Traffiques and Discoveries of the English Nation. London: Chato and Windus (1981) Vol. 6, 318-323.

157. Hanke, Lewis. The Spanish Struggle for Justice in the Conquest of America. Philadelphia: Univ. of Pennsylvania Press (1949).

158. Harris, C.H. The Spanish Empire in America. New York: Oxford Univ. Press (1947).

159. Helms, Mary W. and Franklin O. Loveland, eds. Frontier Adaptations in Lower Central America. Philadelphia: ISHI (1976).

160. Humphreys, R.A. and John Lynch, eds. The Origins of the Latin American Revolutions 1808-1826. New York: Knopf (1965).

161. Humphreys, R.A. Economic Aspects of the Fall of the Spanish American Empire. 30 Revista de Historia de America 450 (December 1950).

162. Hussey, Roland D. Text of the Laws of Burgos (1512-1513) Concerning the Treatment of the Indians. 12 HAHR 301 (1932).

163. Ladd, Doris M. The Mexican Nobility at Independence 1780-1826. Austin: Univ. of Texas (1976).

164. Lanning, John Tate. Academic Culture in the Spanish Colonies. New York: Oxford Univ. Press (1940).

165. Larson, Magali Sarfatti. Spanish Bureaucratic-Patrimonialism in America. Berkeley: Univ. of Cal. Press (1966).

166. Lewy, G. Constitutionalism and Statecraft during the Golden Age of Spain. Geneva: Droz (1960).

167. Lockhart, James. Spanish Peru 1532-1560. Madison: Univ. of Wisconsin Press (1968).

168. ______ and Enrique Otte, eds. Letters and People of the Spanish Indies Sixteenth Century. Cambridge: Cambridge Univ. Press (1976).

169. Loveman, Brian. Chile: The Legacy of Hispanic Capitalism. New York: Oxford Univ. Press (1979).

170. Lynch, John. The Spanish-American Revolutions, 1808-1826. New York: W.W. Norton (1976).

171. ______________. Spanish Colonial Administration, 1782-1810: The Intendant System in the Viceroyalty of Rio de la Plata. University of London Historical Studies, 5. London: Athlone Press (1958).

172. MacLachlan, Colin M. Criminal Justice in Eighteenth Century Mexico. Berkeley: Univ. of Cal. Press (1974).

173. ______________, and Jaime E. Rodríguez O. The Forging of the Cosmic Race: A Reinterpretation of Colonial Mexico. Berkeley: Univ. of Cal. Press (1980).

174. Madden, M.R. Political Theory and Law in Medieval Spain. N.Y.: Fordham Univ. Press (1930).

175. Margadant, Guillermo Floris. An Introduction to the History of American Law. Trans. Eugenia Ursua-Cocke. 3d ed. Dobbs Ferry: Oceana (1983).

176. Martin, Luis. The Kingdom of the Sun: A Short History of Peru. New York: Scribner (1974).

177. McAlister, Lyle N. The Fuero Militar in New Spain Gainesville: Univ. of Florida Press (1957).

178. ______________. Social Structure and Social Change in New Spain. 43 HAHR 349 (1963).

179. Means, Philip A. Indian Legislation in Peru. 3 HAHR 509 (1920).

180. Moore, John P. The Cabildo in Peru under the Hapsburgs. Durham: Duke Univ. Press (1954).

181. ______________. The Cabildo in Peru under the Bourbons. Durham: Duke Univ. Press (1966).

182. Morales Padrón, Francisco. Las leyes nuevas de 1542-1543. Anuario de estudios Americanos 561 (1959).

183. Moreno, The Spanish Colonial System: A Functional Approach. 20 Western Pol. Q. 308 (1967).

184. Morse, Richard M. Toward a Theory of Spanish American Government. 15 J. Hist. Ideas 71 (1954).

185. Note. Legal Relations in Afro-Indian Relations in Colonial Mexico. 55 J. Negro Hist. 131 (1970).

186. O'Gorman, Edmundo. The Invention of America. Bloomington: Indiana Univ. Press (1961).

187. Ots Capdequí, José María. Historia del Derecho Español en América y del Derecho Indiano. Madrid: Aguilar (1967).

188. ____________________. Instituciones sociales de la América española en el período colonial. Buenos Aires: La Plata (1934).

189. ____________________. Estudios de la Historia del Derecho Español en las Indias. Bogotá: Editorial Minerva, S.A. (1940).

190. ____________________. Manual de Historia del Derecho Español en las Indias. Buenos Aires Editorial Losada, S.A. (1945).

191. Padden, Robert C. The Hummingbird and the Hawk: Conquest and Sovereignty in the Valley of Mexico: 1503-1541. Columbus: Ohio State Univ. Press (1967).

192. Parkes, Henry Bamford. A History of Mexico. 3rd ed. Boston: Houghton Mifflin (1969).

193. Parry, J.H. The Sale of Public Office in the Spanish Indies under the Hapsburgs. Berkeley: Univ. of Cal. Press (1953).

194. ____________________. The Audiencia of Galicia in the Seventeenth Century. Cambridge: Cambridge Univ. Press (1948).

195. ____________________. The Spanish Theory of Empire in the Sixteenth Century. Cambridge: The University Press (1940).

196. ____________________, and Philip Sherlock. A Short History of the West Indies. 3rd ed. New York: St. Martin's Press (1971).

197. Payne, S. G. A History of Spain and Portugal. Madison: Univ. of Wisconsin Press (1973).

198. Pendle, George. A History of Latin America. Middlesex: Penguin Books (1980).

199. Phelan, J. L. The Kingdom of Quito in the Seventeenth Century: Bureaucratic Politics in the Spanish Empire. Madison: Univ. of Wisconsin Press (1967).

200. Picón-Salas, Mariano. A Cultural History of Spanish America: From Conquest to Independence. Trans. Irving A. Leonard. Berkeley: Univ. of Cal. Press (1962).

201. Pizarro, Pedro. Relation of the Discovery and Conquest of the Kingdom of Peru, ed. P.A. Means. New York: Cortes Soc'y (1921).

202. Powell, P. W. Soldiers, Indians and Silver: The Northwest Advance of New Spain 1550-1600. Berkeley: Univ. of Cal. Press (1952).

203. Prado, Caio Jr. The Colonial Background of Modern Brazil. Trans. Suzette Macedo. Berkeley: Univ. of Cal. Press (1971).

204. Prescott, William. History of the Conquest of Peru. New York: Harper Bros. (1847).

205. Renan, Ernest. Caliban. Trans. Eleanor Grant Victory. New York: The Shakespeare Press (1896).

206. Roberts-Wray, K. Commonwealth and Colonial Law. New York: Praeger (1966).

207. Rowe, John H. The Incas Under Spanish Colonial Institutions. 37 HAHR 155 (1957).

208. Rodo, Jose Enrique. Ariel. Caracas: Biblioteca Ayacucho (1976).

209. Sahagún, Bernardino de. Florentine Codex: General History of the Things of New Spain. Trans. Arthur J. O. Anderson & Charles E. Dibble. Santa Fe: Univ. of Utah and School of American Research (1950-1975).

210. Sancho, Pedro. An Account of the Conquest of Peru. Trans. P. A. Means. New York: Cortes Society (1917).

211. Sánchez Albornoz, Claudio. Spain: A Historical Enigma. Trans. C.J. Dees & D.S. Reher. Madrid: Fundación Universitaria Española (1979).

212. Santistevan, J. La huelga en el Perú. Historia y Derecho. Lima: CEDES (1981).

213. Sariola, Sakari. Power and Resistance: The Colonial Heritage of Latin America: Ithaca: Cornell Univ. Press (1972).

214. Sarmiento, Domingo F. Life in the Argentine Republic in the Days of the Tyrants: or Civilization & Barbarism. New York: Hafner (1971).

215. Saver, Carl O. The Early Spanish Main. Berkeley: Univ. of Cal. Press (1966).

216. Simpson, Lesley B. The Encomienda in New Spain: The Beginning of Spanish Mexico. Rev. ed. Berkeley Univ. of Cal. Press (1966).

217. ____________________. Studies in the Administration of the Indians in New Spain. Berkeley: Univ. of Cal. Press (1934).

218. Smith, M.G. The Plural Society in the British West Indies. Berkeley: Univ. of Cal. Press (1965).

219. Smith, Robert S. Legal Foundations of the Spanish Consulado. 48 Jurid. Rev. 147 (1936).

220. Soberanes Fernandes, José Luis. Los tribunales de la Nueva España. México: UNAM (1980).

221. Spurdle, Frederick G. Early West Indian Government Private Publication by the Author, 44 Russell St., Palmerston North, New Zealand (1962).

222. Stein, Stanley J. and Barbara H. Stein. The Colonial Heritage of Latin America: Essays on Economic Dependence in Perspective. New York: Oxford U. Press (1970).

223. Stevens, Henry A. and F.W. Lucas, Trans. The New Laws of the Indies. London: Chiswick Press (1893)

224. Sweet, David G. and Gary B. Nash, eds. Struggle and Survival in Colonial America. Berkeley: Univ. of Cal. Press (1981).

225. Symposium. Colonial Institutions of Contemporary Latin America. 43 HAHR 371 (1963).

226. Tannenbaum, Frank. Ten Keys to Latin America. New York: Viking Books (1960).

227. Taylor, William B. Drinking, Homicide and Rebellion in Colonial Mexican Villages. Stanford: Stanford Univ. Press (1979).

228. Tripoli, C. Historia do Direito Brasileiro. Sao Paulo: Revista dos Tribunaes (1936).

229. Vance, J.T. The Background of Hispanic-American Law: Legal Sources and Judicial Literature of Spain. Washington, D.C.: Catholic Univ. Press (1937).

230. Véliz, Claudio. The Centralist Tradition of Latin America. Princeton: Univ. Press (1980).

231. Villamarín, Judith E. Indian Labor in Mainland Spanish America. Newark: Univ. of Delaware (1975).

232. Walton, Clifford. The Civil Law in Spain and Spanish America. Washington: W.H. Lowdermilk & Co. (1900).

233. Wiedner, Donald L. Forced Labor in Colonial Peru 16 The Americas 357 (1960).

234. Woodward, Ralph Lee, Jr. Central America: A Nation Divided. New York: Oxford Univ. Press (1976).

235. Worcester, Donald E. The Spanish American Past. Enemy of Change. 11 J. Inter-Am. Stud. 66 (Jan. 1969).

236. Zavala, Silvio. The Political Philosophy of the Conquest of America. México: Editorial Cultura (1953).

# II. VARIETIES OF LEGAL EXPERIENCE IN LATIN AMERICA: THE INTERPLAY OF POLITICS, ECONOMICS, IDEOLOGY, & CONVENTION

## A. Thought, Legal Thought, and Styles of Legal Reasoning

237. Blachman, Morris J. and Ronald G. Hellman, eds. Terms of Conflict: Ideology in Latin American Politics. Philadelphia: ISHI (1977).

238. Correas, O. Introducción a La Crítica del Derecho Moderno. Puebla: UNAP-UNAG (1982).

239. Crawford, William R. A Century of Latin American Thought. Cambridge: Harvard Univ. Press (1961).

240. Cumberland, Charles C. Mexico: The Struggle for Modernity. New York: Oxford Univ. Press (1968).

241. Davis, Harold Eugene. The History of Ideas in Latin America. 3 Latin American Res. Rev. 23 (Fall, 1968).

242. ________. Sources and Characteristics of Latin American Thought. Topic 20. Washington and Jefferson College, (Fall, 1970), p. 12.

243. ________. Latin American Thought: A Historical Introduction. Baton Rouge: Louisiana State Univ. Press (1972).

244. Fix Zamudio, Héctor. "La Ciencia del Derecho en el Ultimo Siglo: México," in M. Rotondi Inchieste di DiRitto comparato (6), 460-501. Padova: Cedam (1976).

245. Humphreys, R.A. and John Lynch, eds. The Origins of the Latin American Revolutions, 1808-1826. New York: Knopf (1965).

246. Kaplan, Marcos. Teoría Política y Realidad LatinoAmericana. México: Fondo de Cultura Económica (1976).

247. Klein, Lucia M. Gomes. A Nova Ordem Legal e a Redefinicao Das Bases De Legitimidade. Master's

Thesis, Conjunto Universitario Candido Mendes, Rio De Janeiro (1973).

248. Kunz, Josef L., ed. Latin American Legal Philosophy. Cambridge: Harvard Univ. Press (1948).

249. Paz, Octavio. The Labyrinth of Solitude: Life and Thought in Mexico. Trans. Lysander Kemp. New York: Grove Press (1961).

250. Pérez Perdomo, Rogelio. Ensayo de Periodization De La Historia Social del Derecho en Venezuela. 2 Libro Homenaje a Jose Melich Orsini 703 (1983).

251. Phelan, John L. The Millennial Kingdom of the Franciscans in the New World. Berkeley: Univ. of Cal. Press (1970).

252. Picón-Salas, Mariano. A Cultural History of Spanish America: From Conquest to Independence. Trans. Irving A. Leonard. Berkeley: Univ. of Cal. Press (1962).

253. Sarmiento, Domingo F. Life in the Argentine Republic in the Days of the Tyrants; or Civilization and Barbarism. New York: MacMillan (1868).

254. Silva Herzog, Jesús. El Pensamiento Económico, Social y Politico de México 1810-1964. Mexico: Fondo de Cultura Económica (1967).

255. Villegas, Abelardo. Reformismo y Revolución en el Pensamiento Latinoamericano. 5th ed. México: Ed. Siglo XXI (1980).

256. Williams, Edward J. Latin American Political Thought: A Developmental Perspective. Tucson: Univ. of Arizona Press (1974).

257. Zea, Leopoldo. The Latin American Mind. Trans. James H. Abbott and Lowell Durham. Norman, Okla.: Univ. of Oklahoma Press (1963).

## 1. General: Modes of Legal Analysis

258. Benavente, William. Panorama de la filosofía jurídica en Chile. Santiago de Chile: Editorial jurídica de Chile (1969).

259. Blachman, Morris J. and Ronald G. Hellman, eds. Terms of Conflict: Ideology in Latin American Politics. Philadelphia: ISHI (1977).

260. Butte, Woodfin L. "Stare Decisis, Doctrine and Jurisprudence in Mexico and Elsewhere," in Joseph Dainow, ed., The Role of Judicial Decisions and Doctrine in Civil Law and in Mixed Jurisdictions. Baton Rouge: Louisiana State Univ. Press (1974).

261. Canales, J.T. Important Differences in Our Jurisprudence and The Roman or Civil Law. 11 Texas B.J. 579 (1948).

262. Carrio, Genaro R. Judge-made Law under a Civil Code. 41 LA. L. Rev. 992 (1981).

263. Casad, R.C. Unjust enrichment in Argentina: common law in a civil law system. 22 Am. J. Comp. L. 757 (1974).

264. Delgado Ocando, José M. Lecciones de Filosofía Del Derecho. Maracaibo: U. Nacional del Zulia, (1957).

265. Davis, Harold E. Legal and Political Thought in Mexico. 8 Inter-Am. L. Rev. 95 (1966).

266. Eder, Phanor J. A Comparative Survey of Anglo-American and Latin American Law. New York: NYU Press (1950).

267. __________. "Common and Civil Law Concepts in the Western Hemisphere," in Washington Society of Comparative Law, ed., A Symposium of the Law on Latin America, p. 1 (1959).

268. Esquivel Pérez, Javier. Kelsen y Ross, formalismo y realismo en la Teoría del Derecho. México: UNAM (1980).

269. Fix-Zamudio, Héctor. Some Aspects of Constitutional Interpretation in Mexico's Legal System. 11 Comp. Jur. Rev. 105 (1974).

270. Guandique, José S. Problemas entorno a la norma jurídica. Proyecciones. San Salvador: Ministerio de cultura (1957).

271. Means, Robert A. Underdevelopment and the Development of Law: Corporations and Corporations Law in Nineteenth Century Colombia. Chapel Hill: Univ. of No. Car. Press (1980).

272. Newman, Ralph A. Trust, Civil Law Concepts and Legal Realism. 3 Inter-Am. L. Rev. 379 (1961).

273. Nuñez, Manuel. El Lenguaje Jurídico y sus implicaciones en la Ciencia del Derecho. 17

Revista de la Facultad de la Universidad de Madrid 557 (No. 48, 1973).

274. Pérez-Perdomo, Rogelio. El Formalismo Jurídico y sus Funciones Sociales en el Siglo XIX Venezolano. Caracas: Monte Avila (1978).

275. Puertas-Gómez, Gerardo. El Precedente Judicial y la Jurisprudencia en los Sistemos Jurídicos Norteamericano y Mexicano. Tesiss, Universidad de Monterrey, Div. de Ciencias Jurídicas (March, 1981).

276. Recaséns-Siches, Luis, et al. Latin American Legal Philosophy. Trans. Gordon Ireland et al. Cambridge: Harvard Univ. Press (1948).

277. Reisman, V. Michael. Book Review, 29 Am. J. Comp. Law. 727 (1981).

278. Register, L.B. The Dual System of Civil and Commercial Law. 61 U. Pa. L. Rev. 240 (1912).

279. Rusis, Armins. The Influence of Roscoe Pound on Contemporary Jurisprudence. 5 Inter-Am. L. Rev. 411 (1963).

280. Soler, Sebastián N. Ley, Historia y Libertad. Buenos Aires: Losada (1943).

281. Taylor, H. The Jurisprudence of Latin America: The Fusion of Roman and English Law in the New World. 1 Virginia L. Rev. 1 (1913).

282. Vasconcelos, José. A Mexican Ulysses. Trans. Wm. Rex Crawford. Bloomington: Univ. of Indiana Press (1963).

283. Winizky, Ignacio. Reflections on Legislative Techniques -- Some Teachings Derived from Comparative Law. 2 Inter-Am. L. Rev. 389 (1960).

284. Wroe, S. New Efforts toward the Indexing, Digesting and Classifying of Legislation and Jurisprudence in Costa Rica. 5 Lawyer of the Americas 240 (1973).

285. Zea, Leopoldo. "Latin American Thought and Social Reality," in M.D. Forkosch, ed., Essays in Legal History in Honor of Felix Frankfurter. Indianapolis: Bobbs-Merril (1966), 253.

## 2. The Influence of Liberalism and Positivism


286. Alberdi, Juan Bautista. Bases y puntos de partida Para la organización política de la Republica Argentina. Buenos Aires: Editorial Universitaria (1966).

287. Aldridge, A. Owen. The Ibero-American Enlightenment. Urbana, Ill.: Univ. of Ill. Press (1971).

288. Ardao, Arturo. Espiritualismo y Positivismo en el Uruguay. México: Fondo de Cultura Económica (1950).

289. Bader, Thomas. Early Positivist Thought and Ideological Conflict in Chile. 26 The Americas 376 (April, 1970).

290. Bastos, Tocary Assis. O positivismo e a realidade brasileira. Belo Horizonte: Universidade de Minas Gerais (1965).

291. Belaúnde, Víctor Andrés. Bolívar and the Political Thought of the Spanish American Revolution. Baltimore: John Hopkins Univ. Press (1938).

292. Bello, Andrés. Obras completas. Santiago: Univ. of Chile (1930-1935).

293. Burns, E. Bradford. The Enlightenment in Colonial Brazil. 25 Journal of the History of Ideas 430 (July-September, 1964).

294. Cockcroft, James D. Intellectual Precursors of the Mexican Revolution, 1900-1913. Austin: Univ. of Texas Press (1968).

295. Cruz Costa, João. A History of Ideas in Brazil. Trans. Suzette Macedo. Berkeley: Univ. of Cal. Press (1964).

296. Cunha, Euclydes da. Rebellion in the Backlands. Chicago: Univ. of Chicago Press (1970).

297. Echeverría, Esteban. Dogma Socialista. LaPlata: prol. Alberto Palcos (1940).

298. Frühling, Hugo. Liberalismo y Derecho Durante el Siglo XIX en Chile, in Ensayos. Santiago: Editora Debates Ltda. (1978).

299. García Laguardia, Jorge M. La Reforma Liberal en Guatemala. México: UNAM (1980).

300. García Máynez, Eduardo. Positivismo Jurídico, Realismo Sociológico y Iusnaturalismo. Mexico: Textos Universitarios (1977).

301. Hale, Charles A. Mexican Liberalism in the Age of Mora, 1821-1853. New Haven: Yale Univ. Press (1968).

302. Irving, T.B. "On the Enlightenment in Central America," in A.O. Owen, ed., The Ibero-American Enlightenment. Urbana, Ill.: Univ. of Ill. Press (1971).

303. Jaramillo, J. El Pensamiento Colombiano en El Siglo XIX. Bogotá: Temis (1964).

304. Kilgore, W.J. The Development of Positivism in Latin America. 19 Inter-Am. Rev. of Bibl. 23 (April-June, 1979).

305. Lynch, John, ed. The Origins of the Latin American Revolutions, 1808-1826. New York: Morton (1973).

306. Monteiro de Barros Leas, Iván. Historia de positivismo no Brasil. Sao Paulo: Compania Editora Nacional (1960).

307. Moses, Bernard. The Intellectual Background of the Revolution in South America, 1810-1824. New York: Hispanic Society of America (1926).

308. Noriega, Alfonso. El pensamiento conservador y el conservadurismo mexicano. México: UNAM (1972).

309. Northrop, F.S.C. Ideological Differences and World Order. Studies in the Philosophy and Science of the World's Cultures. New Haven: Yale Univ. Press (1949).

310. Pierson, W.W., ed. The Pathology of Democracy in Latin America. 44 American Political Science Review 100 (1950).

311. Pike, Frederick B. Hispanismo, 1898-1936: Spanish Conservatives and Liberals and Their Relation with Spanish America. Notre Dame: Univ. of Notre Dame Press (1971).

312. Raat, William O. Leopoldo Zea and Mexican Positivism, An Appraisal. 48 HAHR 441(February, 1968).

313. Reyes Heroles, Jesús. El liberalismo mexicano. 3 vols. México: UNAM (1957-1961).

314. Rodó, José E. Ariel. Trans. F.U. Stimson. Boston: Houghton Mifflin (1922).

315. Sampay, Arturo Enrique. La Filosofía del Iluminismo y la Constitución Argentina de 1852. Buenos Aires: Editorial Depalma (1944).

316. Schmitt, Karl M. The Mexican Positivists and the Church-State Question, 1876-1911. 8 J. Church & State 200 (1966).

317. Scott, James Brown. Francisco Suárez: His Philosophy of Law and of Sanctions. 22 Geo. L. J. 405 (1934).

318. Seabra Fegundes, M. Democratic Legality. 4 Lawyer of the Americas 44 (1972).

319. Soler, Ricuarte. El positivismo Argentino. Panamá: Imprenta Nacional (1959).

320. Trazegnies, Fernando de. La idea de Derecho en el Perú Republicano del siglo XIX. Lima: Pontificia Universidad Católica (1979).

321. Tulchin, Joseph S., ed. Problems in Latin American History: The Modern Period. New York: Harper & Row (1973).

322. Whitaker, A.P., ed. Latin America and the Enlightenment. 2d ed. Ithaca: Cornell Univ. Press (1942).

323. __________. Changing and Unchanging Interpretations of the Enlightenment in Spanish America. 114 Proceedings of the American Philosophical Society 256 (August, 1970).

324. Zea, Leopoldo. Apogeo y decadencia del Positivismo en México. México: El Colegio de México (1944).


3. Socialism and Marxism as Driving Forces in Revolutionary Legal Thought


325. Aguilar, Luis E., ed. Marxism in Latin America. Rev. ed. Philadelphia: Temple Univ. Press (1978).

326. Alexander, Robert J., ed. and trans. Aprismo: The Ideas and Doctrines of Víctor Raúl Haya de la Torre. Kent, Ohio: Kent State Univ. Press (1973).

327. Alexander, Robert J. The Communist Party of Venezuela. Stanford: Hoover Institute Press (1969).

328. _________. Communism in Latin America. New Brunswick: Rutgers Univ. Press (1957).

329. Allende-Gossens, Salvador. Nuestro Camino al Socialismo-- La Vía Chilena. Buenos Aires: Ediciones Papiro (1971).

330. Allman, T.D. Rising to Rebellion. Harper's (March, 1981) p. 31.

331. Alvarez Tabío, Fernando. Politica Y Legalidad. Habaña: Editorial Ciencias Sociales (1977).

332. _______________. Política Y Derecho Internacional. Habaña: Editorial Ciencias Sociales (1978).

333. Anderson, Thomas. Matanza: El Salvador's Communist Revolt of 1932. Lincoln: Univ. of Nebraska Press (1971).

334. Azicri, Max. The Governing Strategies of Mass Mobilization: The Foundations of Cuban Revolutionary Politics. 2 Sind J. Pol. Sci. and Modern History 1 (Winter, 1976).

335. _________. A Cuban Perspective on Socialist Legality. 6 Rev. Soc. L. 203 (1980).

336. _________. An Introduction to Cuban Socialist Law. 6 Rev. Soc. L. 153 (1980).

337. Bains, John M. Revolution in Peru: Mariátegui and the Myth. University, Alabama: Univ. of Alabama Press (1972).

338. Berman, Harold J. and Van R. Whiting, Jr. Impressions of Cuban Law. 28 Am. J. Comp. L. 475 (1980).

339. Bernardo, Robert M. The Theory of Moral Incentives in Cuba. Montgomery: Univ. of Alabama (1971).

340. Bishop, Maurice. Forward Ever! Sydney: Pathfinder Press (1982).

341. Bonachea, Rolando and Nelson P. Valdés, eds. Cuba in Revolution. Garden City: Doubleday (1972)

342. Brady, James P. Fresh Winds on Rotted Sails: Spanish Legal Reforms, American Parallels, and the Cuban Socialist Alternative. 9 Intl. J. Soc. L. 177 (May, 1981).

343. Calderio, Francisco (Blas Roca). Los fundamentos del socialismo en Cuba. Habana: Ediciones Populares (1960).

344. Cantor, Robert. New Laws for a New Society. 8 Cuban Resource Center Newsletter, No. 5-6 (December, 1973).

345. Carvalhosa, Modesto. Cuba's 1976 Socialist Constitution and the Fidelista Interpretation of Cuban Constitutional History. 55 Tulane L. Rev. 1223 (1981).

346. Castro, Fidel. Balance de la Revolucioń. México: Ediciones Culturas Popular (1976).

347. __________. Fidel Castro Speaks. Ed. Martin Kenner and James Petras. New York: Grove Press (1969).

348. __________. Selected Works of Fidel Castro. Ed. Rolando Bonachea and Nelson Valdés. Cambridge: MIT Press (1972).

349. __________. Discursos En Tres Congresos. Habaña: Editorial Politica (1982).

350. __________. Our Power Is that of the Working People. Fidel Castro Speeches II, ed. Michael Taber. New York: Pathfinder Press (1983).

351. Dixon, Marlene and Susanne Jonas, Eds. Revolution and Intervention in Central America. San Francisco: Synthesis Publications (1982).

352. Cea Egana, José Luis. Law and Socialism in Chile, 1970-1973. Ph.D. Diss., Univ. of Wisconsin (1979).

353. Chaliand, Gerard. Revolutions in the Third World. New York: Viking Press (1977).

354. Che Guevara Speaks: Selected Speeches and Writings. Ed. George Lavan. New York: Pathfinder Press (1967).

355. Clissold, Stephan, ed. Social Relations with Latin America, 1918-1968. London: Oxford Univ. Press (1970).

356. Davis, Harold Eugene. Latin American Social Thought. Washington, DC: University Press of Washington (1961).

357. Debray, Regis. The Chilean Revolution: Conversations with Allende. New York: Pantheon Books (1971).

358. __________. Revolution in the Revolution? Trans. Bobbye Ortiz. New York: Grove Press (1976).

359. __________. The Revolution on Trial. London: Penguin (1978).

360. __________. Che's Guerilla War. Trans. Rosemary Sheed. Baltimore: Penguin (1975).

361. Domínguez, Jorge I. Cuba: Order and Revolution. Cambridge: Harvard Univ. Press (1978)

362. Draper, Theodore. Castroism: Theory and Practice. New York: Praeger (1965).

363. __________. Castro's Revolution. New York: Praeger (1962).

364. Fernández Retamar, Roberto, Caliban. Habaña: Editorial Arte y Literatura (1979).

365. The First Socialist Constitution in the Americas. 3 Center for Cuban Studies Newsletter 36 (March-June, 1976).

366. Gerassi, John ed. Venceremos: The Writings and Speeches of Ernesto Che Guevara. London: Weidenfeld & Nicolson (1968).

367. Gettleman, Marvin E., et al., eds. El Salvador: Central America in the New Cold War. New York: Grove Press (1981).

368. Gheerbrant, Alain. The Rebel Church in Latin America. London: Penguin (1974).

369. Gilly, Adolfo. The Mexican Revolution. Trans. Patrick Cammiller. London: Verso (1983).

370. Guevara, Ernesto Che. "Che" Guevara on Revolution. Jay Mallin, ed. Coral Gables: Univ. of Miami Press (1969).

371. __________. Selected Works of Ernesto Che Guevara. Cambridge: MIT Press (1969).

372. __________. "Man and Socialism in Cuba," in Man and Socialism in Cuba, ed. Bertram Silverman. New York: Atheneum (1971).

373. Haya de la Torre, Víctor Raúl. Y después de la Guerra Que? Lima PTCM (1946).

374. __________. Política Aprista. Lima: Editorial Amanta (1967).

375. Herman, Donald L., ed. The Communist Tide in Latin America. Austin: Univ. of Texas Press (1973).

376. Hodges, Donald C. The Latin American Revolution. New York: William Morrow (1974).

377. Horowitz, Irving Louis, ed. Cuban Communism. 4th Ed. New Brunswick: Transaction Books (1981).

378. ___________. Beyond Empire and Revolution: Militarization and Consolidation in The Third World. New York: Oxford Univ. Press (1982).

379. Huberman, Leo and Paul M. Sweezy, eds. Regis Debray and the Latin American Revolution. New York: Monthly Review Press (1968).

380. International Commission of Jurists. Cuba and the Rule of Law. Geneva, XV (1962), p. 267.

381. Kantor, Harry. Aprismo: Peru's Indigenous Political Theory. 53 South Atlantic Q. 1 (1954).

382. __________. The Ideology and Program of the Peruvian Aprista Movement. Rev. ed. Washington: Savile Book Store (1966).

383. Korn, Alejandro. La libertad creadora. Buenos Aires: Losada (1944).

384. Lascher, Iván. Escrito con la Izquierda. Caracas: Libros Teguy (1977).

385. Lewis, Paul H. Socialism, Liberalism and Dictatorship in Paraguay. New York: Praeger (1982).

386. Loveman, Brian. Chile: The Legacy of Hispanic Capitalism. New York: Oxford Univ. Press (1979).

387. Lowenthal, Abraham, ed. The Peruvian Experiment. Princeton: Princeton Univ. Press (1975).

388. Lowy, Michael. The Marxism of Che Guevara. London: Monthly Review Press (1973).

389. Mallea, Eduardo. Historia de una pasión argentina. Buenos Aires: SUR (1937).

390. Mariátegui, José Carlos. Seven Interpretive Essays on Peruvian Reality. Trans. Marjory Urquidi. Austin: Univ. of Texas Press (1971).

391. Martí, José. Obras Completas. Habana: Editorial Lex (1946).

392. Martínez-Estrada, Ezequiel. X-Ray of the Pampa. Trans. Alain Swietlicki. Austin: Univ. of Texas Press (1971).

393. Maynard, Fredelle. Cuba: The Revolutionary Left. 244 The Atlantic Monthly 4 (No. 4, October, 1979).

394. McNicoll, R.E. Intellectual Origins of Aprismo. 23 HAHR 424 (1943).

395. Menéndez Rodríguez, Mario. Voices from El Salvador. San Francisco: Solidarity Publications (1983).

396. Novoa, Eduardo. The Crisis of Law. 2 Boletin del Instituto de Docenia e Investigacion Juridicas 39 (1972).

397. ________. Hacia Una Nueva Conceptualización Jurídica. 15 Cuadernos de la Realidad Nacional 203 (1972).

398. Ordoñez Martínez, Francisco. La Legalidad Socialista, Firme Baluarte De Los Intereses Del Pueblo. Habaña: Editorial Ciencias Sociales (1982).

399. Padilla, H. Fuera del juego. La Habana: Unión de Escritores y Artistas de Cuba (1968).

400. Parilli, R.E.F. Effects of Castroismo and Guevarismo on leftist thought in Latin America. 12 Rev. D.P. 69 (1972).

401. Richards, Eduard B. Marxism and Marxist Movements in Latin America in Recent Soviet Historical Writings. 45 HAHR 577 (1965).

402. Robinson, David A. Peru in Four Dimensions. Lima: American Studies Press (1965).

403. Roca, Blas. Specific Features of Socialist Democracy in Cuba. 20 World Marxist Review, no. 2 (February, 1977).

404. Rojas, Fernando. Controversia Marxista. La teoría de la transición de los modos de producción. Bogotá: CINEP (1978).

405. ________. Marco filosófico de los estudios jurídicos en Colombia. 50 Ideas y Valores 71 (1977).

406. Rosales, J., ed. Legalidad y Poder Popular en Cuba. Buenos Aires: Editorial Convergencia (1976).

407. Saco, Alfredo. Aprista Bibliography. 23 HAHR 55 (1943).

408. Santos, Theotonio D. Socialismo o Fascismo. Mexico: Editorial Edicol (1978).

409. Schneider, Ronald. Communism in Guatemala, 1944-1954. New York: Praeger (1954).

410. Sobre la Justicia en Chile. Santiago: Ediciones Univ. de Valparaíso (1973).

411. Velasco, Juan. La Voz de la Revolución. Lima: Oficina Nacional de Difusión del Sinamos (1972).

412. Viera-Gallo, José A. The Legal System and Socialism. 1972 Wisconsin L. Rev. 686 (1972).

413. Walter, Richard J. The Socialist Party of Argentina, 1890-1930. Austin: Univ. of Texas Press (1977).

414. Weinstein, Martin, ed. Revolutionary Cuba in the World Arena. Philadelphia: ISHI (1979).


## 4. Liberation Theology and the Role of Religion in the Formation of Ideas about Law.


415. Arce Martínez, Sergio. "The Mission of the Church in a Socialist Society," in Religion in Cuba Today. Eds. Alice Hageman and Philip Wheaton. New York: Association Press (1981).

416. Berryman, Phillip. Latin American Liberation Theology. 34 Theological Studies 357 (Sept. 1973).

417. Bruneau, J.C. The Political Transformation of the Brazilian Church. London: Cambridge Univ. Press (1974).

418. Callcott, Wilfred Hardy. Church and State in Mexico 1822-1857. Durham: Univ. of North Carolina Press (1926).

419. Castro, Fidel. Habla Fidel Castro sobre los cristianos revolucionarios. Hugo Assman, ed. Montevideo (1972).

420. "Central America: The Strongmen are Shaking." 7 Latin American Perspectives 190 (Spring-Summer, 1980).

421. Comment: Church and State in Latin America. 8 J. Church & St. 437 (1973).

422. Confederación Latinoamericana de Religiosos (CLAR). La justicia en el mundo: Textos sinodales, aportes de la Iglesia Colombiana. Bogotá: SPEC (1972).

423. Della Cava, Ralph. Catholicism and Society in Twentieth Century Brazil. 11 Latin Am. Res. Rev. 7 (no. 2, 1976).

424. Dewart, Leslie. Christianity and Revolution: The Lesson of Cuba. New York: Herder and Herder (1963).

425. Dodson, Michael. The Christian Left in Latin American Politics. 21 J. Inter-Am., Stud. & World Aff. 45 (February, 1979).

426. Domínguez, Jorge I. Cuban Catholics and Castro. 15 Worldview, no. 2 (February, 1972).

427. Dusell, Enrique. History and the Theology of Liberation: A Latin American Perspective. Trans. John Drury. Maryknoll: Orbis Books (1976).

428. ________. A History of the Church in Latin America: Colonialism to Liberation. Grand Rapids: Eerdmans (1981).

429. Eagleson, John and Philip Scharper, eds. Puebla and Beyond: Documentation and Commentary. Maryknoll: Orbis Books (1979).

430. La Evangelización en el Presente y en el Futuro de América Latina. Puebla: Documento Aprobado (1979).

431. Ferm, Deane W. Contemporary American Theologies: A Critical Survey 54-66. New York: Seabury Press (1981).

432. Gerassi, John, ed. Revolutionary Priest: The Complete Writings & Messages of Camilo Torres. New York: Vintage (1971).

433. Gettleman, Marvin E., et al., eds. El Salvador: Central America in the New Cold War. New York: Grove Press (1981).

434. Gheerbrant, Alain. The Rebel Church in Latin America. London (1974).

435. Gibellini, Rosino, ed. Frontiers of Theology in Latin America. Maryknoll: Orbis Books (1979).

436. Greenleaf, R.E., ed. The Roman Catholic Church in Colonial Latin America. New York: Knopf (1971).

437. Gutiérrez, Gustavo. A Theology of Liberation. Trans. & Ed. Caridad Inda and John Eagleson. Maryknoll: Orbis Books (1971).

438. Hageman, Alice and Philip Wheaton, eds. Religion in Cuba Today: A New Church in a New Society. New York: Association Books (1971).

439. Harper, Charles. Los derechos humanos y la respuesta cristiana en América Latina. 1 Educación Boletín 37 (Lima) (1975).

440. Hobsbawm, E.J. Pact with the Devil. New York Review of Books. September 18, 1980, p.3.

441. Holleran, Mary Patricia. Church and State in Guatema New York: Columbia Univ. Press (1949).

442. Houtart, François and Emile Pis. The Church and the Latin American Revolution. New York: Sheed & Ward (1965).

443. Kennedy, John J. "The Legal Status of the Church in Latin America: Some Recent Developments," in Henry Landsberger, ed., The Church and Social Change in Latin America. Notre Dame: Univ. of Notre Dame Press (1970), 157.

444. Landsberger, H.A., ed. The Church & Social Change in Latin America. Notre Dame: Univ. of Notre Dame Press (1970).

445. Lernoux, Penny. Notes on a Revolutionary Church: Human Rights in Latin America. New York: Alicia Patterson Foundation (1978).

446. Levine, Daniel H. Religion and Politics, Politics and Religion. 21 J. Inter-Am. Stud. 5 (1979), no. 1.

447. ________. Religion and Politics in Latin America: The Catholic Church in Venezuela and Colombia. Princeton: Princeton Univ. Press (1981).

448. ________, ed. Churches and Politics in Latin America. Beverly Hills: Sage Pub. (1980).

449. Lewy, Guenter. Religion and Revolution. New York: Oxford Univ. Press (1974).

450. Magallón-Ibarra, Jorge Mario. El matrimonio. Sacramento, Contrato, Institución. México: Tipografíca Editora Mexicana (1965).

451. Martz, John D. and David J. Myers. Venezuela: The Democratic Experience. New York: Praeger (1977).

452. Míguez-Bonino, José. Doing Theology in a Revolutionary Situation. Philadelphia: Fortress Press (1975).

453. Monroy-Cabra, Marco G. Régimen Concordatorio Colombiano Bogotá: Editorial Temis (1975).

454. Montgomery, Tommie Sue. The Church in the Salvadoran Revolution. 10 Latin American Perspectives (Winter 1983, p.62).

455. Pike, Frederick B. Catholic Church and Modernization in Peru and Chile? 20 J. Inter-Am. Affairs 272 (No. 2 1966).

456. ________. Modernized Church in Peru: Two Aspects. 26 Rev. Pol. 307 (1964).

457. Preston, Julia. Time on the Cross. 2 Democracy, 116 (April, 1982).

458. Riding, Alan. The Sword and the Cross. New York Review of Books, May 28, 1981, p.3.

459. Rodríguez, E. On Religious Freedom in Cuba. Granma Weekly Rev., December 4, 1977, p.6.

460. Rosa, Martín de la. La Iglesia Catolica en México: del Vaticano II a la CELAM (1965-1979). 19 Cuadernos Políticos 88 (Enero-Mayo 1979).

461. Segundo, Juan Luis. The Liberation of Theology. Trans. John Drury. Maryknoll: Orbis Books (1976).

462. Sejourné, Laurette. Burning Water: Thought and Religion in Ancient Mexico. Berkeley: Shambhala (1976).

463. Smith, Brian H. Old Allies, New Enemies: The Catholic Church as Opposition to Military Rule in Chile, 1973-1979. Paper, Workshop on Six Years of Military Rule in Chile, Woodrow Wilson Center, Washington, D.C. (1980).

464. ________________. The Church and Politics in Chile. Princeton: Princeton Univ. Press (1982).

465. Taussig, Michael T. The Devil and Commodity Fetishism in South America. Chapel Hill: Univ. of North Carolina Press (1980).

466. Torres, Camilo. *Revolutionary Writings*. New York: Herder & Herder (1969).

467. Torres, Sergio, Virginia Fallella and John Eagleson, eds. *Theology in the Americas*. Maryknoll: Orbis Books (1976).

468. We Worshipped Idols. 5 *Cuba Rev.* 8 (September, 1975).

469. Wiliman, J. Adalberto Tejada and the Third Phase of the Anti-Clerical Conflict in Twentieth Century Mexico. 15 *J. Church & St.* 437 (1973).

## B. *Codes and Constitutions: Legal Mythologies and Political Reality*

### 1. *Codification: North Atlantic Models and South Atlantic Experience*

470. Benson, Nettie Lee, ed. *Mexico and the Spanish Cortes, 1810-1822: Eight Essays*. Austin: Univ. of Texas Press.

471. Brown, L.N., ed. The Sources of the Spanish Civil Law. 5 *Int'l and Comp L. J.* 364 (July 1956).

472. Canales, J.T. Important Differences in Our Jurisprudence and the Roman or Civil Law. 11 *Texas B.J.* 579, 603 (1948).

473. Carrio, Genard R. Judge-made Law Under a Civil Code. 41 *La. L. Rev.* 993 (1981).

474. Cueto Rúa, Julio C. The Future of the Civil Law, 37 *La.L.Rev.* 645 (1977).

475. De Gasperi, Luis. El Futuro de la Codificación. 29 *Tulane L. Rev.* 223 (1955).

476. Eder, Phanor J. *A Comparative Survey of Anglo-American and Latin American Law*. New York: NYU Press (1950).

477. ______________________. "Common and Civil Law Concepts in the Western Hemisphere," in Washington Society of Comparative Law, ed., *A Symposium of the Law in Latin America* (1959), p. 1.

478. ______________________. The Impact of the Common Law on Latin America. 4 *Miami L. Q.* 435 (1950).

479. Gomes, Orlando. Comments on the Reform of Civil Codes. 5 Inter-Am. L. Rev. 137 (1963).

480. ______________________. Historical and Sociological Roots of the Brazilian Civil Code. 1 Inter-Amer. L. Rev. 331 (1959).

481 ______________________. Renovation of the Brazilian Civil Code. 8 Inter-Am L. Rev. 171 (1966).

482. Kirchberger, Hans. The Significance of Roman Law for the Americas and Its Importance to Inter-American Relations. 1944 Wisc. L. Rev. 249.

483. Kozolchyk, Boris. Commercial Law Recofification and Economic Development in Latin America. 4 Lawyer of the Americas 189 (1972).

484. Lafaille, Héctor. Fuentes del Derecho Civil en América Latina. Buenos Aires: Abelardo-Perrot (1959).

485. Lawson, F.H. A Common Law Lawyer Looks at Codification. 2 Inter-Am. L. Rev. 1 (1960).

486. Matus-Valencia, Juan G. The Centenary of the Chilean Civil Code. 7 Am. J. Comp. L. 71 (1958).

487. Means, Robert C. Codification in Latin America: The Brazilian Commercial Code of 1850. 10 Tex. Int. L. J. 347 (1975).

488. ______________________. Codification in Latin America: The Colombian Commercial Code of 1853. 52 Tex. L. Rev. 18 (1973).

489. Mendonca, Juan Carlos. Legislative Reform in Paraguay and the Renovation of the Civil Code. 6 Inter-Am. L. Rev. 347 (1964).

490. Merryman, John H. The Civil Law Tradition. Stanford: Stanford Univ. Press (1969).

491. Molina Pasquel, R. El Derecho Angloamericano Contemporáneo, Ensayo de Derecho Comparado sobre el Sistema Norteamericano en el Ultimo Cuarto del Siglo. 5 Boletin del Instituto de Derecho Comparado de México 13 (1952).

492. Murray, Daniel E. The New Code of Civil Procedure of Guatemala. 7 Inter-Am. L. Rev. 303 (1965).

493. Nichols, Madaline W. Las Siete Partidas. 20 Cal. L. Rev. 20 (1932).

494. Osterling Parodi, Felipe. Peruvian Civil Code. 14 Lawyer of the Americas 593 (1983).

495. Scott, Samuel P. (ed.) Las Siete Partidas 960-963. Chicago: Commerce Clearing House (1931).

496. Valencia, Matus. The Centenary of the Chilean Civil Code. 7 Am. J. Comp. L. 71 (1958).

2. Constitutionalism, Personalismo, and the Military: The Tragi-Comedy of High Formality in Latin American Law

497. Abranches, Sergio H. and Glaucio A. Dillon Soares, Las Funciones del Poder Legislativo. Rev. Latino Americana de Ciencia Política, No. 2, Agosto (1972).

498. Allman, T.D. Rising to Rebellion. Harper's, March 1981, p.31.

499. Ameringer, Charles D. Democracy in Costa Rica. New York: Praeger (1982).

500. Anderson, Charles W. "El Salvador: The Army as Reformer," in Martin C. Needler, ed., Political Systems of Latin America. Princeton: Van Nostrand (1964), p. 53.

501. ________________. Politics and Economic Change in Latin America: The Governing of Restless Nations. Princeton: Van Nostrand (1967).

502. ________________. "The Somoza Dynasty," in Political Systems of Latin America, ed. Martin C. Needler. New York: Van Nostrand Reinhold. 2d ed. (1970).

503. Armstrong, Robert and Janet Shenk. El Salvador: The Face of Revolution. Boston: South End Press (1982).

504. Ayearst, Morley. The British West Indies: The Search for Self-Government. New York: NYU Press (1960).

505. Azicri, Max. Change and Institutionalization in the Revolutionary Process: Cuba in the 1970's. 6 Rev. Soc. L. 164 (1980).

506. ____________________. The Institutionalization of the Cuban Revolution: A Review of the Literature. 9 Cuban Studies/Estudios Cubanos 63 (July 1979).

507. ______________. The Institutionalization of the Cuban State: A Political Perspective. 22 J. Interam. Stud. & World Affairs 315 (No. 3, 1980).

508. ______________. "Introduction" to The Constitutions of the Communist World: Cuba. Amsterdam: Sijthoff & Noordhoff (1980).

509. Barbosa, Ruy. Constituicao Federal Brasilieira. Sao Paulo: Livraria Academia (1933).

510. Barker, W.F. and C.N. Ronning. Internal Security and Military Power: Counter-insurgency and Civic Action. Columbus: Ohio State Univ. Press (1966).

511. Batiza, Rodolfo. Legal and Political Aspects of Statism in Mexico. 4 Inter-Am. L. Rev. 139 (1962).

512. Berry, Albert, Ronald G. Hellman and Mauricio Solaun, eds. Politics of Compromise: Coalition Government in Colombia. New Brunswick: Transaction Books (1980).

513. Black, Jan Knippers, Howard I. Blutstein, et al. Area Handbook for Cuba. Washington: U.S. Govt. Printing Office (1976).

514. Blankstein, George J. Ecuador: Constitutions and Caudillos. New York: Russell & Russell (1964).

515. Bolívar, Simón. Address to the Angostura Congress, February, 1819 in Selected Writings of Bolívar. Ed. Vicente Lecuna. Trans. & Ed. Harold A. Bierck, Jr. Caracas & New York: Colonial Press (1951).

516. Boorstein, Edward. Allende's Chile: An Inside view. New York: Int'l Publishers (1977).

517. Brill, William. Military Intervention in Bolivia: The Overthrow of Paz Estensoro and the MNR. Washington: Institute for the Study of Political Systems (1967).

518. Buenes, Luz, et al. Normas Fundamentales del Estado de Chile. Santiago: Ediciones Jurídicas (1975).

519. Bulnes Ripamonti, Christian. Relaciones y Conflictos entre los Organos del Poder Estatal. Santiago: Editorial Universitaria (1965).

520. Burgoa, Ignacio. Derecho Constitucional Mexicano. México: Editorial Porrúa (1982).

521. Burns, E. Bradford. Latin America: A Concise Interpretive History. 3d edition. Englewood Cliffs: Prentice Hall (1982).

522. Busey, J. Observations on Latin American Constitutionalism. 24 The Americas 46 (1967).

523. Caballero, Ricardo. Yrigoyen: la conspiración civil y militar del 4 de febrero de 1905. Buenos Aires: Editorial Raigal (1951).

524. Camp, Roderick A. Mexican Political Biographies, 1935-1975. 2d ed. Tempe: Univ. of Arizona Press (1982).

525. Campodonico, Francisco, ed. La Nueva Constitucion y su Aplicacion Legal. 9 Ensayos Criticos. Lima: Centro De Investigación y Capacitación (1980).

526. Campos-Harriet, Fernando. Historia Constitucional de Chile. 5th ed. Santiago: Editorial Jurídica de Chile (1977).

527. Cardenas, Leonard. Contemporary Problems of Local Government in Mexico. 18 West. Pol. Q. 858 (1965).

528. Cardoso, Fernando Henrique & Enzo Faletto. Estado y Sociedad en América Latina. Buenos Aires: Ediciones Nueva Visión (1972).

529. Carpizo, Jorge. Estudios Constitucionales. México: UNAM (1980).

530. ________________. La Constitución Mexicana de 19 México: UNAM (1979).

531. ________________, ed. Las Experiencias del Proce Político Constitucional en México y Espana. Mexico: UNAM (1979).

532. ________________, and Jorge Madrazo. Derecho Constitucional. México: UNAM (1981).

533. Carvalhosa, M. Cuba's 1976 Socialist Constitution and the Fidelista Interpretation of Cuban Constitutional History. 55 Tulane L. Rev. 1223 (1981).

534. Casal, Lourdes. On Popular Power: The Organization of the Cuban State During the Period of Transition. 2 Latin American Perspectives 78 (Supp. 1975).

535. "Central America: The Strongmen are Shaking." 7 Latin American Perspectives No. 3, 190 (Spring-Summ 1980).

536. "Chile: Blood on the Peaceful Road." 1 Latin American Perspectives no. 2 (Summer 1974).

537. Clark, D. Judicial Protection of the Constitution in Latin America. 2 Hast. Con. L. Q. 405 (1975).

538. Cochran, Charles L. The Estrada Doctrine and U.S. Policy. 5 Lawyer of the Americas 27 (1973).

539. Collier, David, ed. The New Authoritarianism in Latin America. Princeton: Princeton Univ. Press (1979).

540. Collier, Jane. Law and Social Change in Zinacantan Stanford: Stanford Univ. Press (1973).

541. ______________. Political Leadership in Zinacantan. 11 Law and Society Rev. 131 (1976).

542. Comment. The Socialist Constitution of Cuba (1976). 17 Colum. J. Transnat'l L. 451 (1978).

543. Constitución y grupos de presion en América Latina. Instituto de Investigaciones Jurídicas. México: UNAM (1977).

544. Cotayo, Nicolás L. Un Recorrido por el Sistema Penal Cubano. 5 Cuba Internacional 45 (May 1973).

545. Coveman, Brian. Chile: The Legacy of Hispanic Capitalism. New York: Oxford Univ. Press (1979).

546. Cumberland, Charles C. Mexican Revolution: The Constitutionalist years. Austin: University of Texas Press (1972).

547. Dana Montano, S.M. Justicia Social y Reforma Constitucional. Buenos Aires (1949).

548. ________________. The Constitutional Problems of the Argentine Republic. 6 Am. J. Comp. L. 340 (1957).

549. De La Cuesta, Leonel-Antonio. The Cuban Socialist Constitution. 6 Cuban Studies/Estudios Cubanos, No. 1-2, June-July 1976.

550. Democracy and Dictatorship in Latin America. New York: Foundation For The Independent Study of Social Ideas (1982).

551. Denton, Charles. Patterns of Costa Rican Politics. Boston: Allyn Bacon (1971).

552. Diaz Arenas, Pedro A. Estado y Tercer Mundo: El Constitucionalismo. Bogotá: Temis (1980).

553. Domínguez, Jorge. Institutionalization and Civil Military Relations in Cuba. 6 Cuban Studies 39 (January 1976).

554. Dretze, Gottfried. Government of the People: A European Looks at the Americas. 33 Americas, 18 (no. 5 May 1981), p. 18.

555. Duncan W. Raymond. The Mexican Constitution of 1917: Its Political and Social Background. 5 Inter-Am. L. Rev. 277 (1965).

556. Einaudi, Luigi. The Peruvian Military: A Summary Political Analysis. Santa Monica: The Rand Corporation (1969).

557. El Salvador: Background to the Crisis. Cambridge: Central America Information Office (1982).

558. Evans, Peter. Dependent Development: The Alliance of Multinational State, and Private Capital in Brazil. Princeton: Princeton Univ. Press (1979).

559. Ewell, Judith. Indictment of a Dictator: Extradition and Trial of Marcos Pérez Jiménez. Texas A. & M. University Press (1981).

560. Fagen, Richard R. Charismatic Authority and the Leadership of Fidel Castro. 18 West. Pol. Q. 275 (June 1965).

561. The First Party Congress: Institutionalization of the Cuban Revolution. 3 Center for Cuban Studies Newsletter, No. 23 (Mar.-June 1976).

562. The First Socialist Constitution in the Americas. 3 Center for Cuban Studies Newsletter 36 (March-June 1976).

563. Fitch, John S. The Military Coup d'Etat as a Political Process: Ecuador, 1948-1966. Baltimore: Johns Hopkins U. Press (1977).

564. Fitzgibbon, R. Dictatorship and Democracy in Latin America. 36 Int'l Affairs 48 (1960).

565. Fitzgibbon, R. Latin American Constitutions: Textual Citations. Tempe: Center for Latin American Studies, Arizona State Univ. (1974).

566. Fix Zamudio, Héctor. Justicia Constitucional y Régimen Democrático en Iberoamérica. 9 Anuario Jurídico 379 (1982) (Mexico).

567. Fix Zamudio, Héctor. Evolución de la organización político - constitucional en América Latina (1950-1975). México: UNAM (1978).

568. Folsom, V.C. Constitutional Development in the Countries of the Americas. 9 Lawyer of the Americas 495 (1977).

569. Gallón-Giraldo, Gustavo. Quince años De stado de sitio n Colombia: 1958-1978. Bogotá: Libreria Editorial A.L. (1979).

570. García Laguardia, Jorge M. Partidos Políticos y Democracia en Iberoamérica. México: UNAM (1980).

571. ________________________. Orígenes de la Democracia Constitucional en Centroamérica. San José: Editorial Universitaria Centroamérica. 2d ed. (1976).

572. Garcia-Menéndez, Alberto A. "Estructura Jurídica del Castrismo," in Carlos A. Montaner, ed., Diez Años de Revolución Cubana. San Juan (1970), p. 59.

573. García Pelayo, Manuel, et al. Constitución Y Grupos de Presión En America Latina. México: UNAM (1977).

574. Gelard. Le Procesus d'Institutionnalisation de la Republique de Cuba. 43 Notes et Etudes Documentaires 7 (Documentation Francaise Feb. 15, 1977).

575. Gettleman, Marvin E., et al., eds. El Salvador: Central America in the New Cold War. New York: Grove Press (1981).

576. Gil, Federico G. The Political System of Chile. Boston: Houghton Mifflin (1966).

577. Gil, Federico G., Ricardo Lagos, Henry A. Landsberger. Trans. John S. Gitlitz. Chile at the Turning Point. Philadelphia: ISHI (1979).

578. Gil-Valdivia, Gerardo & Jorge Chávez Tapia. Evolución de la Organización Político-Constitucional en América Latina. México: UNAM (1978).

579. Gil Yepes, José Antonio. El reto de las élites. Madrid: Editorial Tecnos (1978).

580. Gilmore, Robert. Caudillism and Militarism in Venezuela, 1810-1910. Athens: Ohio University Press (1964).

581. Gilmore, William C. The Associated States of the Commonwealth Caribbean: The Constitutions and the Individual. 11 Lawyer of the Americas 1 (1979).

582. Glejeses, Piero. The Dominican Crisis, 1965 Constitutionalist Revolt, and American Intervention. Baltimore: Johns Hopkins (1979).

583. González, Carlos E. Bases para una democracia social:gobierno constitucional o poder militar? Buenos Aires: S. Rueda (1980).

584. González, E. The Party Congress and Poder Popular: Orthodoxy, Democratization, and the Leader's Dominance. 6 Cuban Studies/Estudios Cubanos 1 (No. 2 July 1976).

585. González Casanova, Pablo. La Democracia en México. 12th ed. México: Ediciones Eros. (1980).

586. González Navarro, Moisés. Anatomía del poder, 1848-1853. México: El Colegio de México (1977).

587. Grimes, W.W. Mexico's Constitution. 11 J. Bar Assoc. D.C. 116 (1944).

588. Grondona, Mariano. Los dos poderes. Buenos Aires: EMECE Editores (1973).

589. Hamilton, Nora. The Limits of State Autonomy: Post-Revolutionary Mexico. Princeton: Princeton Univ. Press (1982)

590. Handelman, Howard and Thomas G. Sanders, ed. Military Government and the Movement Toward Democracy in South America. Bloomington: Indiana Univ. Press (1981).

591. Harnecker, Marta, ed. Cuba: Dictatorship or Democracy? Westport: Lawrence Hill & Co. (1979).

592. Hennessey, Alistair. "Fascism and Populism in Latin America," in Walter Laqueur, ed., Fascism: A Reader's Guide. Berkeley: Univ. of Cal. Press (1976).

593. Horowitz, Irving Louis. Cuban Communism. 3d ed. New Brunswick: Transaction Books (1977).

594. ____________. Military Origins of Third World Dictatorship and Democracy. 3 Third World Quarterly 38 (1981).

595. __________. Political Legitimacy and the Institutionalization of Crises in Latin America. 1 Comp. Pol. Stud. 1 (April 1968).

596. Hazard, John N. The Common Core of Marxian Socialist Constitutions. 19 San Diego L. Rev. 297 (1982).

597. Ilsley, L.L. The Argentine Constitutional Revolution of 1949. 14 Journal of Politics, no. 2 (1952), p. 224.

598. Imaz, José Luis de. Los que Mandan. Buenos Aires: Editorial Universitaria de Buenos Aires (1964).

599. Int'l Com. of Jurists. Cuba and the Rule of law. Vol. XV. Geneva (1962), p. 267.

600. Johnson, John J. The Military and Society in Latin America. Stanford: Stanford Univ. Press (1964).

601. ________, ed. The Role of the Military in Underdeveloped Countries. Princeton: Princeton Univ. Press (1972).

602. ________. Political Change in Latin America. Stanford: Stanford Univ. Press (1958).

603. La Feber, Walter. Inevitable Revolutions. The Atlantic Monthly. June 1982, p. 74.

604. Lambert, Jacques. Latin America: Social Structure and Political Institutions. Trans. Helen Katel. Berkeley: Univ. of Cal. Press (1967).

605. Lechner, N., ed. Estado y política en América Latina. México: Siglo XXI (1981).

606. Leo Grande, William M. Oligarchs and Officers: the Crisis in El Salvador. 58 Foreign Affairs 1084.

607. Lernoux, Penny. Latin America: A Political Guide to 33 Nations. 233 The Nation, no. 5 (Aug. 22-29, 1981), 133-148.

608. Lieuwen, Edwin. Arms and Politics in Latin America. New York: Praeger (1960).

609. ________. Generals vs. Presidents: Neo Militarism in Latin America. New York: Praeger (1964).

610. Linares-Quintana, Segundo V. Introducción a la Teoría del poder constituyente. 65 Ley 787 (1957).

611. Linz, Juan J. & Alfred Stepan, eds. The Breakdown of Democratic Regimes in Latin America. Baltimore: Johns Hopkins Univ. Press (1978).

612. Lisbonne, Jean. Le Nouvel Droit de la Republique de Cuba. Rev. int. droit comp. (1976), p. 351.

613. Loveman, Brian. Chile: The Legacy of Hispanic Capitalism. New York: Oxford Univ. Press (1979).

614. ________________. Peru's Ambiguous Revolution. 52 Foreign Affairs 799 (1974).

615. Loveman, Brian and Thomas M. Davies, Jr., eds. The Politics of anti-Politics: The Military in Latin America. Lincoln: Univ. of Nebraska Press (1978).

616. Lowenthal, Abraham F., ed. Armies and Politics in Latin America. New York: Holmes & Meier (1976).

617. Maechling, Charles, J. The Argentine Pariah. Foreign Policy. (Summer, 1982), p. 69.

618. Malloy, James M., ed. Authoritarianism and Corporatism in Latin America. Pittsburgh: Univ. of Pittsburgh Press (1977).

619. Margolles, Pedro. Building Up a System of Representative Bodies. 18 World Marxist Review 60 (no. 2 Feb. 1975).

620. Martz, John D. Central America: The Crisis and the Challenge. Chapel Hill: Univ. of North Carolina Press (1959).

621. ____________. "Guatemala, the Search for Political Identity," in Martin Needler, ed., Political Systems of Latin America. New York: Van Nostrand Reinhold (1970).

622. Martz, John D. and David J. Myers. Venezuela: The Democratic Experience. New York: Praeger (1977).

623. McClintock, Cynthia and Abraham F. Lowenthal, eds. The Peruvian Experiment Reconsidered. Princeton: Princeton Univ. Press (1983).

624. Mexico in the Eighties. 9 Latin American Perspectives, no. 1 (Winter 1982).

625. Migdal, Joel S. Peasants, Politics and Revolution. Princeton: Princeton Univ. Press (1977).

626. Montgomery, Tommie Sue, ed. Mexico Today. Philadelphia: ISHI (1982).

627. Moreno, Francisco J. Justice and Law in Latin America--A Cuban Example. 12 J. Inter-Am. Stud. & World Affairs 76 (July, 1970).

628. Moses, Carl. Judicial Control of the Constitutionality of Legislation in Cuba. Ph.D. Dissertation, Univ. of North Carolina, 1958.

629. Nava Negrette, A. Reformabilidad de la Constitución. 25 Revista de la Facultad de Derecho en México 179 (1975).

630. "New Forms of Democracy. 6 Cuba Review no. 3 (1976).

631. Needler, Martin. Mexican Politics: The Containment of Conflict. New York: Praeger (1982).

632. North, Lisa. Civil-Military Relations in Argentina, Chile and Peru. Berkeley: Institute of International Studies, Univ. of Cal. (1966).

633. Nwabueze, Benjamin O. Constitutionalism in the Emergent States. London: C. Hurst (1973).

634. O'Donnell, Guillermo A. Modernization and Bureaucratic-Authoritarianism: Studies in South American Politics. Berkeley: Univ. of Cal. Press (1979).

635. Osiel, Mark J. The Agonies of Abertura. Dissent, Spring 1983, p. 217.

636. Pacheco, Francisco Antonio. Introducción a la Teoría del Estado. San Jose: Editorial Universidad Estatal A Distancia (1980).

637. Parry, John H., and Philip Sherlock. A Short History of the West Indies. 3d ed. New York: St. Martin Press (1971).

638. Passalaqua. The Cuban Fundamental Law of 1959. 10 Rev. der. puertoriqueño 245 (1970).

639. Pelaéz, Carlos. Estado de Derecho y estado de sitio, la crisis de la Constitución en Colombia. Bogotá: Editorial Temis (1955).

640. Pendle, George. A History of Latin America. Middlesex: Penguin Books (1980).

641. Peralta, Hernán G. El Derecho Constitucional en la Independencia de Costa Rica. San José: Trejos Hermanos (1965).

642. Peralta, M.M. Costa Rica: Its Climate, Constitution, and Resources. London: Straker Bros. & Co. (1873).

643. Pérez Perdomo, Rogelio. El Formalismo Jurídico y Sus Funciones Sociales en el Siglo XIX Venezolano. Caracas: Monte Avila (1978).

644. El Poder Legislativo en América Latina. Instituto de Investigacciones Jurídicas, ed. México: UNAM (1974).

645. Potash, Robert A. The Army and Politics in Argentina, 1928-1945. Stanford: Stanford Univ. Press (1969).

646. ______________. The Army and Politics in Argentina 1945-1962: Peron to Frondizi. Stanford: Stanford Univ. Press (1980).

647. El Predominio del Poder Ejecutivo en Latino América. Mexico: UNAM (1977).

648. Purcell, Susan K. Decision-Making in an Authoritarian Regime: Theoretical Implications from a Mexican Case Study. 26 World Pol. 28 (1973).

649. ______________. The Mexican Profit-Sharing Decision: Politics in an Authoritarian Regime. Berkeley: Univ. of Cal. Press (1975).

650. Reisman, W. Michael. Book Review. 29 Am. J. Comp. L. 727 (1981).

651. Revolución y Legalidad: Problemas del Estado y del Derecho En Chile. Cuadernos de la Realidad Nacional (Dec. 1972) (Chile).

652. Reyna, José Luis and Richard S. Weinert. Authoritarianism in Mexico. Philadelphia: ISHI (1977).

653. Robben, Linda A. Opening Brazil to Democracy? 2 Democracy 91 (July 1982).

654. Roel, Santiago. History of Mexican Constitutional Experience: from Zitacuaro, 1811 to Queretaro, 1917. 4 Calif. West L. Rev. 251 (1968).

655. Roett, Riordan. Return to Democracy? Brazil and the Southern Cone. 3 SAIS Rev. 59 (No. 2) (1983).

656. Rorem, M.D. Mexico's Organic Law of Federal Public Administration--a new structure for modern administration. 2 Hastings Int'l & Comp. L. Rev. 367 (1978).

657. Rosales, Juan, ed. Legalidad y Poder Popular en Cuba. Buenos Aires: Editorial Convergencia (1976).

658. Sampay, Arturo E. La Filosofía del Iluminismo y la Constitución Argentina de 1853. Buenos Aires: Editorial Depalma (1944).

659. Sánchez Viamonte, Carlos. El poder constituyente: Origen y Formación del Constitucionalismo universal y especialmente argentina. Buenos Aires: Editorial Bibliografica Argentina (1957).

660. Santos, Juan Carlos. A Difficult but Humane Job: 9 Questions About Penal Reeducation in Revolutionary Cuba. Granma Weekly Review, June 10, 1973, p. 11.

661. Sariola, Sakari. Power and Resistance: the Colonial Heritage of Latin America. Ithaca: Cornell U. Press (1972).

662. Sarmiento, Domingo F. Comentarios a la Constitución de la Confederación Argentina. Santiago: Impr. de J. Belin (1853).

663. Seabra Fegundes, M. Democratic Legality. 4 Lawyer of the Americas 44 (1972).

664. Seco Villalba, José A. Fuentes de la Constitución Argentina. Buenos Aires: Editorial Depalma (1943).

665. Sigmund, Paul E. The Overthrow of Allende and the Politics of Chile 1964-1976. Pittsburgh: Univ. of Pittsburgh Press (1977).

666. Silvert, Kalman H. A Study in Government: Guatemala. New Orleans: Tulane Univ. Press (1954).

667. ________________. National Values, Development, and Leaders and Followers. 16 Int'l Soc. Sci. J. 560 (1964).

668. Smirnow, Gabriel. The Revolution Disarmed: Chile, 1970-1973. New York: Monthly Review Press (1979).

669. Smith, Peter H. Labyrinths of Power: Political Recruitment in Twentieth-Century Mexico. Princeton: Princeton Univ. Press (1979).

670. Snyder, Frederick E. State of Siege and Rule of Law in Argentina: The Politics and Rhetoric of Vindication. 15 Lawyer of the Americas 503 (1984).

671. Spiro, Herbert. Government by Constitution: The Political Systems of Democracy. New York: Random House (1959).

672. Statute on the Rights of Nicaraguans in The Nicaraguan Revolution, eds. Pedro Camejo and Fred Murphy. New York: Pathfinder Press (1979).

673. Steiner, Henry J. and David M. Trubek. Brazil--All Power to the Generals. 49 Foreign Affairs 464 (April 1971).

674. Stepan, Alfred. The Military in Politics: Changing Patterns in Brazil. Princeton: Princeton Univ. Press (1971).

675. ______________. ed. Authoritarian Brazil. New Haven: Yale Univ. Press (1973).

676. __________. The State and Society: Peru in Comparative Perspective. Princeton: Princeton Univ. Press (1978).

677. Stevens, Evelyn P. Legality and Extra-Legality in Mexico. 12 J. Interam. Stud. & World Aff. 62 (1970).

678. Strickon, Arnold and Sidney M. Greenfield, eds. Structure and Process in Latin America: Patronage, Clientage, and Power Systems. Albuquerque: Univ. of New Mexico Press (1972).

679. Sweezy, Paul M. and Harvey Magdoff, eds. Revolution and Counter-Revolution in Chile. New York: Monthly Review Press (1974).

680. Tannenbaum, Frank. The Political Dilemma in Latin America. 38 Foreign Affairs 497 (1959-1960).

681. Therborn, Goren. The Travail of Latin American Democracy. 113-14 New Left Review 71 (1979).

682. Torre Villar, Ernesto de la and Jorge Mario García LaGuardia. Desarollo Historico del Constitucionalismo Hispanomericano. México: UNAM (1976).

683. Torres Santrayll. Antecedentes históricos y principios que informan el Anteproyecto de Constitución [1975]. 10 Revista Cubana de Derecho [Rev. C. Der.] 43.

684. Valadés, Diego. "La Constitución Reformada" in Los Derechos del Pueblo Mexicano 13-191 México: Ed. Manuel Porrũa (1979).

685. __________. La Dictadura Constitucional en América Latina. México: UNAM (1979).

686. Valdés, Nelson, P. Revolution and Institutionalization in Cuba. 6 _Cuban Studies_ 1 (no. 1, July 1976).

687. Valencia Villa, Hernando. _La inconstitucionalidad de la Constitución_. Bogotá: Uniandes (1981).

688. Valencia Carmona, Salvador. _El Poder Ejecutivo Latinoamericano_. México: UNAM (1979).

689. Valenzuela, Arturo. _The Breakdown of Democratic Regimes: Chile_. Baltimore: Johns Hopkins Univ. Press (1978).

690. Vanossi, Jorge Reinaldo A. _Presidencialismo y Parlamentarismo en el Brasil_. Buenos Aires: Cooperadora de Derecho y Ciencias Sociales (1964).

691. Véliz, Claudio, ed. _Obstacles to Change in Latin America_. London: Oxford Univ. Press (1965).

692. Villanueva, Víctor. _El Militarismo en el Perú_. Lima: Empresa Gráfica (1962).

693. Von Krockow, Grof Christian, _Mexiko, Wertschaft Politik Gesellschaft Kultur_. Munich: Piper (1974).

694. Waldmann, Peter and Ernesto Grazón Valdéz, eds. _El Poder Militar en la Argentina 1976-1981_. Buenos Aires: Editorial Galerna (1983).

695. Wiarda, Howard J., ed. _Politics and Social Change in Latin America: The Distinct Tradition_. 2nd ed. rev. Amherst: Univ. of Massachusetts Press (1982).

696. Wiarda, Howard J. _The Continuing Struggle for Democracy in Latin America_. Boulder: Westview Press (1980).

697. ______________. _Politics and Social Change in Latin America_ Amherst: Univ. of Mass. Press (1974).

698. ______________. Toward a Framework for the Study of Political Change in the Iberic-Latin Tradition: The Corporatist Model. 25 _World Politics_ 206 (1973).

699. _______ and Harvey F. Kline, eds. _Latin American Politics and Development_. Boston: Houghton Mifflin (1979).

700. Wynia, Gary W. _Argentina in the Postwar Era_. Albuquerque: Univ. New Mexico Press (1978).

C. Legal Processes: Learning, Living and Delivering Law in Latin America

701. Berman, Harold and Van R. Whiting, Jr. Impressions of Cuban Law. 28 Am. J. Comp. L. 475 (1980).

702. Domínguez, Jorge I. Cuba: Order and Revolution. Cambridge: Harvard Univ. Press (1978).

703. Irons, Peter H. The Relegalization of Cuba. 5 American Legal Studies Association Forum 20 (no. 2 1981).

704. Macaulay, Stewart. Book Review. 29 Am J. Comp. L. 542 (1981).

705. Merryman John H., David S. Clark & Lawrence M. Friedman. Law and Social Change in Mediterranean Europe and Latin America: A Handbook of Legal and Social Indicators for Comparative Study. Stanford: Stanford Law School (1979).

706. Orvalle Favella, José, ed. Temas y Problemas de la Administración de Justicia en Mexico. Mexico: UNAM (1982).

1. Legal Education and Legal Scholarship

707. XL Aniversario del Instituto de Investigaciones Jurídicas. México: UNAM (1980).

708. Baltins, Andris A. The Clinical Education Program of the Universidad de Los Andes. Bogotá: Informe Dactilografiado (1971).

709. Berman, Harold J. and Van R. Whiting, Jr. Impressions of Cuban Law. 28 Am. J. Comp. L. 475 (1980).

710. Bowles, Samuel. Cuban Education and the Revolutionary Ideology. 41 Harvard Educational Review 472 (November 1971).

711. Brown, Brendan F. Recent Significant Trends in Legal Education in the Americas. 3 Inter. Am. L. Rev. 55 (1961).

712. __________. Legal Education in the Americas. 9 J. Legal Ed. 339 (1956).

713. Cuarta Conferencia de Facultades de Derecho. 19 Rev. de Der. Puerto. 255 (1966).

714. "A Educacao Juridica e a Crise Brasileira." 13-14 *Revista Jurídica* 7, 18 (1955).

715. First Conference on Latin American Law Schools. 1 *Inter-Am. L. Rev.* 241 (1959).

716. Gardner, James. *Legal Imperialism: American Lawyers and Foreign Aid in Latin America*. Madison: Univ. of Wisconsin Press (1980).

717. González Orellana, Carlos. *Historia de la educación en Guatemala*. Guatemala: Editorial José de Pineda Ibarra (1970).

718. Guerra Iñíguez, David. *La enseñanza del Derecho en Venezuela*. Caracas: Grafiunica (1978).

719. Harrison, L. Learning and Politics in Latin American Universities. 27 *Proc. Acad. Pol. Sci.* 23 (1964).

720. Headrick, William C. "Introducing the Method of Active Teaching in Latin America: Colombia's First Seminar on Legal Education." 22 *J. Legal Educ.* 333 (1970).

721. Horack, Claude. Legal Education in the Latin American Republics. 3 *J. Legal Ed.* 287 (1950).

722. Huteau, Michel and Jacques Lautrez. *L'éducation à Cuba*. Paris: Maspero (1973).

723. Karol, K.S. *Guerrillas in Power: The Course of The Cuban Revolution*. Trans. Arnold Pomeranz. New York: Hill and Wang (1970).

724. Laing, Edward A. Revolution in Latin American Legal Education: the Colombian Experience. 6 *Lawyer of the Americas*. 370 (1973).

725. Lanning, J.T. *Academic Culture in the Spanish Colonies*. New York: Oxford Univ. Press (1940).

726. Latin American Studies Assoc. Subcomm. on Academic Freedom and Human Rights in Argentina. *A Report on Academic Freedom and Human Rights in Argentina From May 25, 1973 to March 24, 1976*. Occasional Paper no. 21. New York: Ibero-American Language and Area Center, N.Y.U. (1976).

727. Letelier, Valentín, et al. *Reforma de la Enseñanza del Derecho*. Santiago de Chile (1889).

728. Lowenstein, Steven. Lawyers, Legal Education and Development. An Examination of the Process of Reform in Chile. New York: Internat'l Legal Cente (1970).

729. Lynch, Dennis O. Hundred Months of Solitude: Myth or Reality in Law and Development? 1983 Am. B. Found. J. 223 (1983).

730. Madrazo, Jorge. El sistema disciplinario de la Universidad Nacional Autónoma de México. México: UNAM (1980).

731. Martín, Luis and Jo Ann Guerin Pettus, eds. Scholars and Schools in Colonial Peru. Dallas: School of Continuing Education, Southern Methodist University (1973).

732. Maxwell, Richard C. and Marvin G. Goldman. Mexican Legal Education. 16 J. Legal Ed. 155 (1963).

733. Mayda, Jero. Problems of Legal Education in Latin America. 12 J. Legal Ed. 407 (1960).

734. Montano, Jorge. Partidos y Política en América Latina. Mexico: UNAM (1975).

735. Pérez Perdomo, Rogelio. Los Abogados en Venezuela. Caracas: Monte Avila Editores (1981).

736. Primer seminario latinamericano sobre Enseñanza Clínica del Derecho y Asistencia Legal. Santiago d Chile: Universidad Catolica de Chile (1973).

737. Rojas, Fernando. El Problema teórico en la investigación socio-jurídica. 46-47 Ideas y Valore 79 (1976).

738. Roper, Christopher and Jorge Silva. Science and Technology in Latin America. Essex: Longman Group Ltd. (1982).

739. Ruiz Massieu, Francisco. Normación Constitucional de los Partidos Políticos en América Latina. Méxic UNAM (1974).

740. Segunda Conferencia de Facultades de Derecho. XIV Boletín del Instituto de Derecho Comparado de Méxic 555 (1961).

741. Sepúlveda, César. Student Participation in University Affairs: The Mexican Experience. 17 Am. J. Comp. L. 384 (1969).

742. Spencer, David C., ed. Student Politics in Latin America. Philadelphia: U.S. Nat'l Student Ass'n. (1965).

743. Steiner, Henry. Legal Education and Social-Economic Change: Brazilian Perspectives. 19 Am. J. Comp. L. 39 (1971).

744. Tercera Conferencia de Facultades de Derecho. 16 Boletín del Instituto de Derecho Comparado de México, 527 (1963).

745. Vanossi, Jorge Reinaldo. La universidad y sus problemas. Buenos Aires: Ediciones Macci, Club de Estudio (1976).

746. Vargas-Avalos, Pedro. Breve Reseña Histórica de la Faculdad de Derecho de la Universidad de Guadalajara. Guadalajara: Herty (1980).

747. Winterton, George C. Comparative Law Teaching. 22 Am. J. Comp. L. 69 (1975).

748. Wittker V., Jorge, ed. Antología de estudios sobre enseñanza del Derecho. México: UNAM (1976).

## 2. The Legal Profession

749. Arroyo Soto, Augusto. El secreto profesional del abogado y del notario. México: UNAM (1980).

750. Attacks on the Independence of Judges and Lawyers in Argentina. 1 Int'l Com of Jurists Bull. (1978) (entire issue).

751. Balera, Wagner and Santiago Onate. Legal Services for the Poor and Legal Education in Brazil and Mexico. Paper, Law and Society Ass'n, Annual Meeting, Toronto, June 1982.

752. Berman, Harold J. and Van R. Whiting. Impressions of Cuban Law. 28 Am. J. Comp. L. 475 (1980).

753. Clagett, Helen. The Administration of Justice in Latin America. New York: Oceana (1952).

754. Dias, Clarence J. and James C. N. Paul. "Lawyers, Legal Professions, Modernization and Development," in Lawyers in the Third World; Comparative and Developmental Perspectives. Eds. C.J. Dias et al. Upsala: Scandinavian Institute of African Studies and Int'l Center for Law in Development (1981, p. 1). [Hereinafter "Lawyers in the Third World"]

755. Dodd, David, Paul Liebenson and Seymour J. Rubin. The Inter-American Legal Services Association. Promoting the Role of Law in Social Change in Latin America. 12 Lawyer of the Americas 533 (1980).

756. Gardner, James. Legal Imperialism: American Lawyer and Foreign Aid in Latin America. Madison: Univ. o Wis. Press (1980)

757. Headrick, William C. "Introducing the Method of Active Teaching in Latin America: Colombia's First Seminar on Legal Education." 23 J. Leg. Educ 333 (1971).

758. Human Rights in the World: Plight of Defense Lawyers in Argentina. Int'l. Com. of Jurist Rev. (June 1975), p. 1.

759. Klement, Alice. Lawyers Who Remain in Cuba Run Their Practices "Collectively." National Law Journa May 26, 1980, p. 15.

760. Legal Aid and World Poverty. A Survey of Asia, Afri and Latin America. Committee on Legal Services to the Poor in the Developing Countries. New York: Praeger (1974).

761. López Valdéz, Abelardo. Developing the Role of Law in Social Change. 7 Lawyer of the Americas 1 (1975)

762. Lowenstein, Steven. Lawyers, Legal Education and Development: An Examination of the Process of Reform in Chile. New York: Int'l Legal Center (1970).

763. Lynch, Dennis O. Lawyers in Colombia: Perspectives on the Organization and Allocation of Legal Services 13 Texas Int'l L. J. 199 (1978).

764. ____________. Legal Roles in Colombia: Some Social, Economic and Political Perspectives, in Lawyers in the Third World, op. cit., p. 26.

765. _________. Legal Roles in Colombia. Upsala: Upsala Offset Center AB (1981).

766. Margadant, Guillermo Floris. The Mexican Notariate. 6 Cal. West L. Rev. 218 (1970).

767. Murke, D. and J. Fox. The Notaire in North America: A Short Study of the Adaptation of a Civil Law Institution. 50 Tulane L. Rev. 318 (1976).

768. Onate, S. Recent Trends in the Organization of Legal Service in Mexico. Law and Society Association, Annual Meeting, Toronto, June 1982.

769. Palma Fourcade, Anibal. Chile: Proceso de Cambio y Poder Judicial. Paper presented at Colloque International, Le Droit à la Justice et à la Défense dans les Dictadures Militaires en Amérique Latine, Paris, May 28, 1983.

770. Pérez-Perdomo, Rogelio. "Jurists in Venezuelan History," in Lawyers in the Third World, op. cit., p. 76.

771. __________. Los Abogados en Venezuela. Caracas: Monte Avila Editores (1981).

772. Perry, Fred V. Understanding the Mexican Attorney: Legal Education and the Practice of Law in Mexico. 10 Int'l Lawyer 167 (1976).

773. Rojas, Fernando. Descriptions towards Typologies and Analysis of Legal Aid Trends in Latin America. Unpubl. paper, Bogotá, June, 1982.

774. Solano Carrera, Luis F. Prestación de Servicios Legales en Costa Rica. San Jose: Univ. de Costa Rica (1982).

775. Thome, Joseph. New Models for Legal Services in Latin America. University of Wisconsin Law School, Disputes Processing Research Programs, Working Paper 1984-2. Madison, Wis. (1984).

776. Trubek, David. Unequal Protection: Thoughts on Legal Services, Social Welfare, and Income Distribution in Latin America. 13 Texas Int'l L. J. 243 (1978).

## 3. The Judicial Process

### a. Criminal Law and Procedure

777. Akers, R.L., et al. Prisonization in Five Countries. 14 Criminology 527 (1977)

778. Asúa, Luis Jiménez de. I Códigos Penales Iberoamericanos. 8-418 Caracas: Editorial Andrés Bello (1946).

779. __________. I Tratado de Derecho Penal. 1077-1286 Buenos Aires: Editorial Losada (1950).

780. Azicri, Max. Crime and Law Under Socialism: The 1979 Cuban Penal Code. 6 Rev. Soc. L. (1980).

781. Baker, Richard D. Judicial Review in Mexico: A Study of the Amparo Suit. Austin: Univ. of Texas Press (1971).

782. Barona-Labota, J. The Organization of the Police in Mexico. 20 Int'l Rev. Crim. Pol. 218 (1965).

783. Berman, Harold J. & Van R. Whiting, Jr. Impressions of Cuban Law. 28 Am. J. Comp. Law 475 (1980).

784. Brana-Shute, Rosemary and Gary Brana-Shute. Crime and Punishment in the Caribbean. Gainesville: Univ. of Florida Press (1980).

785. Canter, L. Penal Law and Judges in Mexican Jurisprudence. 4 Calif. West. L. Rev. 227 (1968).

786. Clagett, Helen. The Administration of Justice in Latin America. New York: Oceana (1952).

787. Clark, David S. Witchcraft and Legal Pluralism: the Case of Celimo Miquiracama. 15 Tulsa L. J. 679 (1980).

788. Cooper, H.H.A. Law Relating to Sexual Offenses in Peru. 21 Am. J. Comp. L. 86 (1973).

789. ____________. Plea Bargaining: A Comparative Analysis. 5 N.Y.U. J. Int'l L & Pol. 427 (1972)

790. Cruz, Agustín. It took only Three Years: The Destruction of a Law Firm. 50 A.B. A. J. 63 (January 1964).

791. Cuba, Santiago, and Torrado, Osvaldo. El Nuevo Sistema Judicial. 2 Revista Cubana de Derecho 75 (July-Dec. 1973).

792. Eder, Phanor J. "Habeas Corpus Disembodied: The Latin American Experience," in Kurt Nadelman, Arthur T. von Mehren & John Hazard, eds., XXth Century Comparative And Conflicts Law 463. Leyden: A.W. Sijthoff (1961).

793. Fernandez Taboada, Roberto. Quién Es Pedro Nervaiz. Somos, Feb. 11, 1983, p. 6.

794. Garcia Belaunde, Domingo. El Hábeas Corpus en el Peru. Lima: Univ. Nac. Mayor De San Marcos (1979).

795. García Ramírez, Sergio. Derecho penal. México: UNAM (1981).

796. Greve, Frank and Miguel Pérez. Boniato Massacre: What Really Happened? Miami Herald, May 24, 1976, p. 15A.

797. ____________________. Castro's Jails: Still Bulging 17 Years Later. Miami Herald, May 23, 1976, pp. 1, 16A.

798. Gutiérrez, Fela. A Quién Protege el Nuevo Código Penal? Bohemia, June 8, 1979, p. 4.

799. Hurtado Pozo, José. La Ley "Importada": Recepción del Derecho Penal en el Perú. Lima: CEDYS (1979).

800. Irons, Peter H. The Relegalization of Cuba. 5 The American Legal Studies Ass'n. Forum, 20 (no. 2 Winter 1981).

801. Kos-Rabcewicz-Zubkowski, Louis. 1971 Reform to Mexican Penal Code. 4 Lawyer of the Americas 233 (1971).

802. Martínez Pérez, Pedro. Nuevo Sistema Judicial. Cuba International, Nov.-Dec. 1971, p. 72.

803. McDonough, Josefina F. A Transitional Model of the Ecology of Delinquency: The Case of Rio de Janiero. 13 Luso-Brazilian Rev. 138 (no. 2 Winter 1976).

804. Moreno, Francisco J. Justice and Law in Latin America--A Cuban Example. 12 J. Inter-Am. Stud. & World Affairs 376 (July 1970).

805. Murray, Daniel F. Criminal Procedure in the Federal District and Federal Territories of Mexico. 19 Miami L. Q. 251 (1964).

806. ___________. A Comparative Study of Peruvian Criminal Procedure. 21 Univ. of Miami L. Rev. 607 (1967).

807. __________. The Proposed Code of Criminal Procedure of Guatemala. Chicago Comparative Study of the Administration of Justice, Loyola University School of Law (1964).

808. ___________. The Mexican Criminal Jury. 7 Arizona L. Rev. 71 (1965).

809. Petras, James. Chile: Crime, Class Consciousness and the Bourgeoisie. 7 Crime & Soc. Justice 14 (1977).

810. Rico, Jose M. Crime et Justice en Amerique Latine. Montreal: Les Presses de l'Université de Montreal (1978).

811. Rua, Jorge de la. La Codificacion Penal Latinoamericana. Caracas: Universidad Central de Venezuela (1982).

812. Ruiz de Zárate. What does Personal Inviolability Mean? Granma Weekly Rev., August 27, 1978, p. 10.

813. ___________. Is Secrecy of the Mail Protected by Law? Granma Weekly Rev. Jan. 8, 1978, p. 8.

814. Salas, Luis F. Juvenile Delinquency in Postrevolutionary Cuba: Characteristics and Cuban Explanations 9 Cuban Studies/Estudios Cubanos 43 (1979).

815. ___________. The Police as a Social Control Mechanism in Postrevolutionary Cuba. Miami: Florida International Univ. (1979).

816. Schwenk, Edmund Heinz. Criminal Codification and General Principles of Criminal Law in Argentina, Mexico, Chile and the United States: A Comparative Study. 4 La. L. Rev. 351 (1942).

817. Tigar, Michael E. The Educative Function of Criminal Law: Cuban Reforms in Comparative Perspective. National Conference on Cuba. New York, Nov. 1979, Center for Cuban Studies.

818. Valladares, Armando. Prisonero de Castro. ed. Pierre Golendorf. Barcelona: Editorial Planeta (1982).

819. Vallarta, Ignacio. El juicio de Amparo y el Writ of Habeas Corpus México: Impr. F. Díaz de Leon (1881).

820. Zaffaroni, Eugenio Raúl. Política Criminal Latinoamericana: Perspectivas - Disyuntivas. Buenos Aires: Editorial Hammurabi (1982).

b. The Litigation Process

821. Barrios de Angelis, Dante. Teoría del Proceso. Buenos Aires: Ediciones de Palma (1979).

822. Clark, David S. Judicial Protection of the Constitution in Latin America. 2 Hast. Con. L. Q. 405 (1975).

823. _____________. "Witchcraft and Legal Pluralism: The Case of Celimo Miquiracama." 15 Tulsa L. J. 679 (1980).

824. Fix-Zamudio, Héctor and José Ovalle Favela. Derecho Procesal. Mexico: UNAM (1980).

825. Herget, James E. and Jorge Camil. An Introduction to the Mexican Legal System. Buffalo: Wm. S. Hein (1978).

826. International cooperation in civil and commercial procedure: American Continent. Ed. Ludwik Kos-Rabcewics-Zubkowski. Ottawa: Univ. of Ottawa Press (1975).

827. Irons, Peter H. The Relegalization of Cuba. 5 The American Legal Studies Ass'n. Forum 20 (no. 2 Winter 1981).

828. Schwarz, Carl E. Exceptions to the Exhaustion of Administrative Remedies under the Mexican Writ of Amparo: Some possible Applications to Judicial Review in the United States. 7 Calif. West. L. Rev. (1971).

829. Trazegnies, Fernando de. Ciriaco de Urtecho: Litigante por Amor. Lima: Pontificia Universidad Catolica (1981).

c. The Role of the Judiciary

830. Aguilar, Luis E. Cuba 1933, Prologue to Revolution. Ithaca: Cornell Univ. Press, (1972).

831. Argentina: Subjection of the Judiciary. Int'l Com. of Jurists Bull, Sept. 1968, p. 13.

832. Azicri, Max. Change and Institutionalization in the Revolutionary Process: Cuba in the 1970's. 6 Rev. Soc. L. 164 (1980).

833. Baker, Richard R. Judicial Review in Mexico: A Study of the Amparo Suit. Austin: Univ. of Texas Press (1971).

834. Benitez, Illanes. The Supreme Court of Justice of Chile. 7 Int'l Comm. Jurists 264 (1966).

835. Berman, Jesse. The Cuban Popular Tribunals. 69 Calif. L. Rev. 1317 (1969).

836. Berman, Harold J. and Van R. Whiting, Jr. Impressions of Cuban Law. 28 Am. J. Comp. L. 475 (1980).

837. Bielsa, Rafael. "Jurisdictional Protection and Other Remedies Against the Illegal Exercise or Abuse of Administrative Authority," in United

Nations, Remedies Against the Abuse of Adminstrative Authority - Selected Studies 33. (1964).

838. Biles, Robert E. The Position of the Judiciary in the Political Systems of Argentina and Mexico. 8 Lawyer of the Americas 287 (1976).

839. Bock, Philip. K. ed. "The Role of the Court in Rural Mexico," in Philip Bock, ed., Peasants in the Modern World. Albuquerque: Univ. of New Mexico Press (1969).

840. Butte, Woodfin L. "Stare Decisis, Doctrine and Jurisprudence in Mexico and Elsewhere," in Joseph Dainow, ed., The Role of Judicial Decisions and Doctrine in Civil Law and in Mixed Jurisdictions Baton Rouge: Louisiana State Univ. Press (1974).

841. Cabrera, Lucio and W.C. Headrick. Notes on Judicial Review in Mexico and the United States. 5 Inter-Am. L. Rev. 253 (1963).

842. Camargo, Pedro Pablo. The Right to Judicial Protection: Amparo and Other Latin American Remedies for the Protection of Human Rights. 3 Lawyer of the Americas 191 (1971).

843. ____________. The Claim of "Amparo" in Mexico; Constitutional Protection of Human Rights. 6 Calif. West. L. Rev. 201 (1970).

844. Cantor, Robert. New Laws for a New Society. 8 Cuba Resource Center Newsletter, no. 5-6 (Dec. 1973).

845. Carrio, G.R. "Judge-made law under a Civil Code," [Argentina] 41 La. L. Rev. 993 (1981).

846. Clagett, Helen L. The Mexican Suit of "Amparo." 33 Georgetown L. J. 418 (1945).

847. Clark, David S. Judicial Protection of the Constitution in Latin America. 2 Hast. Con. L. Q. 405 (1975).

848. Comité Central del Partido Comunista de Cuba. Comisión de Estudios Jurídicos. Organos del sistema judicial. Habana: Empresa de Medios de Progaganda (1975).

849. Cooper, H.H.A. Peru's "New Look" Judiciary. 55 Judicature 334 (1972).

850. Cuneo, Andrés. La Corte Suprema de Chile. Paper, Fifth Latin American Conference on Law and Development. San José, Costa Rica, August, 1980.

851. Dainow, Joseph, ed. The Role of Judicial Decisions and Doctrine in Civil Law & Mixed Jurisdictions Baton Rouge: Louisiana State Univ. Press (1974).

852. Dirección Nacional de los Tribunales Populares. Manual de los Tribunales Populares. Habana: Ministerio de Justicia, 1966.

853. Donaldson, Diana S. The Costa Rica Amparo in the Period 1950-62. 8 Lawyer of the Americas 371 (1976).

854. Dunshee de Abranches, Carlos. The Inter-American Court of Human Rights. 30 American U.L. Rev. 79 (1980).

855. Eder, Phanor H. Judicial Review in Latin America. 21 Ohio St. L. J. 570 (1960).

856. Feinrider, Martin. Judicial Review and the Protection of Human Rights under the Military Governments in Brazil and Argentina. 5 Suffolk Transnat. L. J., 171 (1981).

857. Fix-Zamudio, Héctor. A Brief Introduction to the Mexican Writ of Amparo. 9 Calif. Western Int'l L. J. 306 (1979).

858. ________. The Writ of Amparo in Latin America. 13 Lawyer of the Americas 361 (1981).

859. _____. "Judicial Protection of the Individual Against the Executive in Mexico," in 2 Gerichtschutz Gegen die Exekutive 713, H. Mosler ed. (1970).

860. ______________, ed. Función del Poder Judicial en los sistemas constitucionales latinoamericanos. México: UNAM (1979).

861. Flory, T. Judge and Jury in Imperial Brazil, 1808 - 1897: Social Control and Political Stability in the New State. Austin: Univ. of Texas Press (1981).

862. Frühling, Hugo. Poder Judicial y Política en Chile. Programa de la Facultad Latinoamericana de Ciencias Sociales, Santiago, Chile (August 1980).

863. Furnish, Dale B. and Roberto MacLean. Court and Statute Law in Peru. 28 Am. J. Comp. L. 487 (1980).

864. Galin, Pedro. La "Independencia" del Poder Judicial Argentino en la Dictadura 1976-1980. Paper, Fifth

Latin American Conference on Law and Development, San José, Costa Rica, August 1980.

865. Garciá Belaúnde, Domingo. El Constitucionalismo Peruano y sus Problemas, Lima: Pontificia Universidad Católica del Perú, Programa Académic de Derecho (1970).

866. Garro, Alejandro. The Role of the Argentine Judiciary in Controlling Governmental Action Under a State of Seige. 4 Human Rights L. J. 311 (1983).

867. Grant, J.A.C. Judicial Control of the Constitutionality of Statutes and Administrative Legislation in Colombia: Nature and evolution of the Present System. 23 So. Calif. L. Rev. 484 (1950).

868. Greue, Frank, and Miguel Pérez. Heavy Political Tones Dominate Style of Justice under Castro. Miami Herald, May 24, 1976, pp. 1, 14-A.

869. Gutiérrez-Gutiérrez, Carlos José. Los jueces de Costa Rica. 22 Revista de Ciencias Jurídicas (Costa Rica) 71 (1973).

870. Harnecker, Marta, ed. Cuba: Dictatorship or Democracy? Westport: Lawrence Hill & Co. (1979).

871. Headrick, William C. Notes on Judicial Review in Mexico and the United States. 5 Inter-Am. L. Rev. 253 (1963).

872. ________. Book Review of Lucio Cabrera, El Poder Judicial Federal Mexicano y el Constituyente de 1917 17 Am. J. Comp. L. 120 (1969).

873. Hunt, Eva and Robert Hunt. "The Role of Courts in Rural Mexico," in Philip Bock, ed., Peasants in the Modern World. Albuquerque: Univ. of New Mexico Press (1969).

874. Ietswaart, Heleen F.P. Labor Relations Litigation: Chile, 1970-1972. 16 Law & Soc'y Rev. 625 (1982).

875. International Commission of Jurists. Cuba and the Rule of Law. vol. xv. Geneva, 267 (1962).

876. Irons, Peter H. The Relegalization of Cuba. 5 The American Legal Studies Ass'n. Forum, 20 (No. 2 Winter 1981).

877. Lessa, Pedro. Do Poder Judiciario. S. Paolo, Bello Horizonte: F. Alves (1915).

878. Lochridge, Edwin P. The Role of the Andean Court in Consolidating Regional Integration Efforts. 10 Georgia J. Int'l L. 351 (1980).

879. Martínez Pérez, Pedro. Nuevo sistema judicial. 3 Cuba internacional no. 28 (December 1971).

880. Menéndez. The Judicial Power and the Constitution [Cuba] Comp. Jur. Rev. (1965), 37-89 and 91-142.

881. Moniz de Aragao, E.D. The Brazilian Judicial Organization. 6 Inter-Am. L. Rev. 239 (1964).

882. Moreno, Francesco J. Justice and Law in Latin America: A Cuban Example. 12 Journal of Inter-American Studies and World Affairs 37 (July 1970).

883. Moses, Carl Calvin. Judicial Control of the Constitutionality of Legislation in Cuba. Ph.D. dissertation, Univ. of North Carolina (1958).

884. Nadorff, Norman J. Habeas Corpus and the Protection of Civil and Political Rights in Brazil: 1964-1978. 14 Lawyer of the Americas 297 (1982).

885. Note. The Writ of Amparo: A Remedy to Protect Constitutional Rights in Argentina. 31 Ohio St. L. J. 831 (1970).

886. Padilla, David J. The Judicial Resolution of Legal Disputes in the Integration Movements of the Hemisphere. 11 Lawyer of the Americas 75 (1979).

887. Pásara, Luis. La Crisis de los jueces peruanos, 6 Apuntes (Perú), No. 11 (1981), p. 3.

888. ________________. Jueces, Justicia y Poder en el Perú. Lima: CEDYS (1982).

889. Rosenn, Keith. Judicial Review in Latin America. 35 Ohio St. L. J. 785 (1975).

890. Santiago Cuba. Los Tribunales en el período de construcción del socialismo. 9 Rev. Cub. Jur. 19 (1962).

891. Scheman, L. Ronald. The Social and Economic Origins of the Brazilian Judges. 4 Inter-Am. L. Rev. 45 (1962).

892. ______. Brazil's Career Judiciary. 46 J. Am. Soc'y Int'l L. 134 (1962).

893. Schwarz, C. Judges under the Shadow: Judicial Independence in the United States and Mexico. 3 Calif. West. L. J. 260 (1973).

894. Seabra Fagundes, Miguel. O Contrôle dos atos administrativos pelo poder judiciaro. Rio de Janeiro: Freitas Bastos (1941).

895. Snow, P.G.: Judges & Generals: The Role of the Argentine Supreme Court during Periods of Military Government. 24 Jahrb. des Offentl. Rs. doz Geg. 609 (1975).

896. Snyder, Frederick E. State of Siege and Rule of Law in Argentina: The Politics and Rhetoric of Vindication. 15 Lawyer of the Americas 503 (1984).

897. Tena-Ramírez, Felipe. The International Expansion of the Mexican Amparo. 1 Inter-Am. L. Rev. 163 (1959).

898. Trueba-Urbina, Alberto & Jorge Trueba-Barrera, eds. Nueva Legislación de Amparo: Doctrina, textos y jurisprudencia. Mexico City: Editorial Porrúa, S.A. (1980).

## 4. Non-Judicial Modes of Dispute Settlement

899. Arnold, V.L. and J. Hamilton. "The Greene Settlement: A Study of the Resolution of Investment Disputes in Peru, 13 Tex. Int. L. J., 263 (1978).

900. Berman, Jesse. The Cuban Popular Tribunals. 69 Calif. L. Rev. 1317 (1969).

901. Bolton, Ralph. To Kill a Thief: A Kallawaga Sorcery Session in the Lake Titicaca Region of Peru. 69 Anthropos, No. 1, 2 (1974), 191-215.

902. Cardenal, Ernesto. In Cuba. Trans. Donald A. Walsh. New York: New Directions (1974).

903. Chagnon, Napoleon A. Yanomamo: The Fierce People. 2d ed. New York: Holt, Rinehart & Winston (1977).

904. Chaudhary, R.L. and G.C. Reid. An Appraisal of the Jamaica Labor Relations and Disputes Act. 8 Lawyer of the Americas 36 (1975).

905. Collier, Jane. Law and Social Change in Zinacantan. Stanford: Stanford Univ. Press. (1973).

906. Future of Arbitration in Latin America: A Study of Its Regional Development. 8 Case Western Res. J. Int'l L. 480 (1976).

907. Gantz, D.A. Dispute Settlement. 73 Proc. A.S.I.L. 249 (1974).

908. Goldman, Marvin G. Arbitration in Inter-American Trade Relations: Regional Market Aspects. 7 Inter-Am. L. Rev. 67 (1963).

909. Hunt, Eva and Robert Hunt. "The Role of Courts in Rural Mexico," in Philip Bock, ed., Peasants in the Modern World. Albuquerque: Univ. of New Mexico Press (1969).

910. Ietswaart, Heleen. "The Discourse of Summary Justice on the Discourse of Popular Justice: An Analysis of Legal Relations in Argentina" in Richard Abel, ed., 2 The Politics of Informal Justice 149. New York: Academic Press (1982).

911. _________. Labor Relations Litigation: Chile, 1970-1972. 16 Law & Soc'y Rev. 625 (1982).

912. _________. Popular Courts in Chile. 30 Nat'l Lawyers Guild Prac. 37 (1973).

913. Macauley, Stewart. Access to the Legal Systems of the Americas: Informal Process. Madison: University of Wisconsin, Working Paper 16 (April 1976).

914. Merieux, M. de. The Ombudsman in the Commonwealth Caribbean. 10 Anglo-Am. L. Rev. 11 (1981).

915. Nader, Laura. Dispute Settlement and Community Organizations: Shii Moslem and Mexican Zapotec (1973).

916. _________, and Duane Metzger. Conflict Resolution in Two Mexican Communities 65 Am. Anthropologist 584 (1963).

917. Payne, James L. Labor and Politics in Peru: The System of Political Bargaining. New Haven: Yale Univ. Press (1965).

918. Rosenn, Keith. The Jeito: Brazil's Institutional Bypass of the Formal Legal System and Its Developmental Implications. 19 Am. J. Comp. L. 526 (1971).

919. Santiago Cuba. Los Tribunales en el período de construcción del Socialismo. 9 Rev. Cub. jur. 19 (1962).

920. Spence, Jack. Institutionalizing Neighborhood Courts: Two Chilean Experiences. 13 Law & Soc'y Rev. 139 (1978, Fall).

921. _________. Search for Justice: Neighborhood Courts in Allende's Chile. Boulder: Westview Press (1979).

922. Summers, L. State Arbritration and Latin America. 3 Calif. Western Int. L. J. 1 (1973).

923. Wesley, R.C. Procedural Malaise of Foreign Investment Disputes in Latin America: from Local Tribunals to Factfinding. 7 Law & Pol. Int'l Bus. 813 (1975).

# III. DREAMS OF VINDICATION: REVOLUTIONARY AND OTHER RESPONSES TO THE RAVAGES OF DEPENDENCY AND THE CHALLENGES OF DEVELOPMENT

## A. Introductory: Theories of Dependence and the Shame of Underdevelopment

924. Aguilar, Alonso, et al. Capitalismo, Atraso y Dependencia en América Latina. 2d ed. México: UNAM (1980).

925. Aguilar, Norma, ed. The Structure of Brazilian Development. New Brunswick: Transaction Books (1979).

926. Barth, Richard and James Dilmus. Dependency Analysis of Latin America: Some Criticisms 11 Latin Am. Res. Rev. 3 (1976).

927. Barty, S.L. The United States & The Development of South America 1945-1975. N.Y.: New Viewpoints (1975)

928. Bishop, Maurice. Forward Ever! Sydney: Pathfinder Press (1982).

929. Bledel Enrique E. The Latin American Development Process and New Legislative Trends. 10 Georgia J. Int'l. L. 325 (1980).

930. Boorstein, Edward. Allende's Chile: An Inside View. New York: Int'l. Publishers (1977).

931. Booth, David. "Andre Gunder Frank: An Introduction and Appreciation," in Ivar Oxaal, Tony Barnett, David Booth, Eds. Beyond The Sociology of Development: Economy and Society in Latin America and Africa. London: Routledge and Kegan Paul (1975).

932. Burg, Elliot M. Law and Development: A Review of the Literature and a Critique of "Scholars in Self-Estrangement." 25 Am. J. Comp. L. 492 (1977).

933. Burns, E. Bradford. Latin America: A Concise Interpretive History. 3d ed. Englewood Cliffs: Prentice Hall (1982).

934. Calvert, Peter. La Revolución Mexicana 1910-1914. México: Ed. El Caballito, S.A. (1978).

935. Cardoso, Fernando H. and Enzo Faletto. Dependency and Development in Latin America. Trans. Marjory M. Urquidi. Berkeley: Univ. of Calif. Press (1979).

936. Cardoso, Fernando H. Dependency and Development in Latin America. 74 New Left Review (July-August. 1972) 83.

937. ___________. The Consumption of Dependency Theory in the United States, 12 Latin Am. Res. Rev. 7 (1977).

938. "Chile: Blood on the Peaceful Road." 1 Latin American Perspectives, no. 2 (Spring-Summer 1980).

939. Cockroft, J., Andre Gunder Frank and D. Johnson. Dependence and Underdevelopment (1972).

940. Davis, Ralph. The Rise of the Atlantic Economies. Ithaca: Cornell Univ. Press (1973).

941. Dependency and Marxism. 8 Latin American Perspectives, no. 3 and 4 (Fall 1981).

942. dos Santos, Teodosio. "The Crisis of Development Theory and the Problem of Dependence in Latin America," in Henry Bernstein, Ed., Underdevelopment and Development: The Third World Today. Harmondsworth: Penguin Books (1973).

943. ___________. The Structure of Dependence. 60 Am. Econ. Rev. 231 (1970).

944. Epstein, Edward C. Introduction to Recent Developments in Mexican Law: Politics of Modern Nationalism. 14 Denver J. of Int. L. and Pol., no. 1 (Spring 1974).

945. Evans, Peter. Dependent Development: The Alliance of Multinational State, and Local Capital in Brazil. Princeton: Princeton Univ. Press (1979).

946. Fagen, Richard R. Studying Latin American Politics: Some Implications of a Dependencia Approach. 12 Latin Am. Res. Rev. 3 (1977).

947. Fernández, Florestán. La Revolución Burguesa en Bra México: Ed. siglo xxi (1978).

948. Fitzpatrick, Peter. Law, Modernization and Mystification. 3 Res. in L. & Soc. 161 (1980).

949. Frank, Andre Gunder. Lumpenbourgeoisie, Lumpen-development: Dependence, Class and Politics in Latin America. New York: Monthly Review Press (1978).

950. _________. Capitalism and Underdevelopment in Latin America. New York: Monthly Review Press (1969).

951. __________. Dependent Accumulation and Under-development. London: Macmillan (1978).

952. Fuentes-Mares, José. La Revolución Mexicana. México: Ed. Contrapuntos-Joaquín Mortiz (1978).

953. Furtado, Celso. Economic Development of Latin America. Trans. Suzette Macedo. 2d ed. London: Cambridge Univ. Press (1976).

954. Gerassi, John. The Great Fear in Latin America. New York: Macmillan (1963).

955. Germani, Gino, et al. Populismo y Contradicciones de clase en Latino América. Mẽxico: Serie Popular Era (1977).

956. Ghosh, Pradip K., ed. Developing Latin America: A Modernization Approach. Westport, CT.: Greenwood Press (1984).

957. Gilly, Adolfo, et. al. Interpretaciones de la Revolución Mexicana. México: Ed. Nueva Imagen UNAM (1979).

958. Gil, Federico, et al., eds. Chile at the Turning Point. Trans. John S. Gitlitz. Philadelphia: ISHI (1979).

959. Greenberg, David G. Law and Development in Light of Dependency Theory. 3 Res. in L. & Soc. 129 (1980).

960. Harding, Timothy F. Dependency, Nationalism and the State in Latin America. 3 Latin American Perspectives 3 (Fall 1978).

961. Hewlett, Sylvia Ann & Richard S. Weinert, eds. Brazil and Mexico: Patterns in Late Development. Philadelphia: ISHI (1982).

962. Hodges, Donald C. Argentina, 1943-1976: The National Revolution and Resistance. Albuquerque: Univ. of New Mexico Press (1976).

963. Humphreys, R. A. and John Lynch, eds. The Origins of the Latin American Revolutions 1808-1826. New York: Knopf (1965).

964. Ianni, Octavio. La Formación del Estado Populista en América Latina. México: Serie Popular Era (1980).

965. Jackson, Steven. An Assessment of Empirical Research on "Dependencia." 14 Latin America Research Review 3 (1979).

966. Kahl, Joseph A. Modernization, Exploitation and Dependency in Latin America: Germani, Gonzalez Casanova, and Cardoso. New Brunswick: Transaction Books (1976).

967. Keohane, Robert O. and Joseph S. Nye. Power and Interdependence: World Politics in Transition. Boston: Little, Brown (1977).

968. Leiken, Robert S. Eastern Winds in Latin America. 42 Foreign Policy 94 (Spring 1981).

969. Leys, Colin. Underdevelopment and Dependency: Critical Notes. 7 J. Contemp. Asia 92 (1977).

970. López-Valdéz, Abelardo. Developing The Role of Law in Social Change: Past Endeavors and Future Opportunities in Latin-America and the Caribbean. 7 Lawyer of the Americas 1 (1975).

971. Loveman, Brian. Chile: The Legacy of Hispanic Capitalism. New York: Oxford Univ. Press (1979).

972. Lynch, John. The Spanish-American Revolutions, 1808-1826. New York: W. W. Norton (1976).

973. Magdoff, Harry. The Age of Imperialism. New York: Monthly Review Press (1969).

974. Malpica Silva-S., Carlos. Los Dueños del Perú. 10th Lima: Ediciones Peisa (1978).

975. Martz, John D. and David J. Myers. Venezuela: The Democratic Experience. New York: Praeger (1977).

976. McClintock, Cynthia and Abraham F. Lowenthal, eds. The Peruvian Experiment Reconsidered. Princeton: Princeton Univ. Press (1983).

977. Merryman, John H. Comparative Law and Social Change: On the Origins, Style, Decline and Revival of the Law and Development Movement. 25 Am. J. Comp. L. 457 (1977).

978. "Mexico in the Eighties." 9 Latin American Perspectives, no. 1 (Winter 1982).

979. Nash, June and Juan Corradi, Eds. Ideology and Social Change in Latin America. New York: June Nash, Juan Corradi and Hobart Spalding, Jr. (1977).

980. Novak, Michael. Why Latin America Is Poor. The Atlantic Monthly, March 1982, p. 66.

981. O'Brien, Philip. "A Critique of Latin American Theories of Dependence," in Oxaal et al., Beyond the Sociology of Development. London: Routledge and Kegan Paul (1975).

982. O'Connor, James. The Origins of Socialism in Cuba. Ithaca: Cornell Univ. Press (1970).

983. Pearce, Jenny. The European Challenge: Europe's New Role in Latin America. London: Latin American Bureau (1982).

984. Pendle, George. A History of Latin America. Middlesex: Penguin Books (1980).

985. Pierre-Charles, Gerard. Génesis de la Revolución Cubana. 2d. ed. México: Ed. Siglo xxi (1978).

986. Platt, D. C. M. Dependency in Nineteenth-Century Latin America. 15 Latin American Res. Rev. 1 (1980).

987. Prebisch, Raúl. The Economic Development of Latin America and Its Principal Problems. Lake Success: UN Dept. of Economic Affairs, ECLA (1950).

988. Raat, William Dirk, ed. Mexico: From Independence to Revolution, 1810-1910. Lincoln: Univ. of Nebraska Press (1982).

989. Ruggiero, Kristin. Gringo & Creole: Foreign and Native Values in a Rural Argentine Community. 24 J. Inter-Am. Study of World Affairs 163 (1982).

990. Sanders, Barry A. The New Mexican Industrial Development Plan. 14 International Lawyer, no. 4 (Fall 1980).

1000. Smirnow, Gabriel. La Revolución Desarmada. Chile. México: Serie Popular Era (1977).

1001. Solomon, Lewis D. Developing Nations and Commercial Banks: The New Dependency. 12 J. Int'l L. & Econ. 325 (1978).

1002. Stepan, Alfred, ed. Authoritarian Brazil. New Haven: Yale Univ. Press (1973).

1003. ___________. The State and Society. Princeton: Princeton Univ. Press (1978).

1004. Sunkel, Osvaldo. The Development of Development Thinking. 8 Int'l Devel. Stud. Bull. 6 (March 1977).

1005. Trubek, David and Marc Galanter. Scholars in Self-Estrangement: Some Reflections on the Crisis in Law and Development Studies in the United States. 1974 Wisconsin L. Rev. 1062 (1974).

1006. Urquidi, Víctor. The Challenge of Development in Latin America. London: Paul Mall Press (1964).

1007. Valenzuela, Arturo and J. Samuel Valenzuela, eds. Chile: Politics and Society. New Brunswick: Transaction Books (1976).

1008. Véliz, Claudio. The Centralist Tradition of Latin America. Princeton: Princeton Univ. Press (1980).

1009. Villamil, José J., ed. Transnational Capitalism and National Development: New Perspectives on Dependence. Hassocks, Sussex: Harvester Press (1979).

1010. Villoro, Luis. El Proceso Ideológico de la Revolución de Independencia. México: UNAM (1981).

1011. Wionczek, Miguel. Inversión y Tecnología Extranjera en América Latina. Mexico: Ed. Joaquin Mortiz (1971).

1012. Wolf, E.R. and Eric C. Hansen, eds. The Human Condition in Latin America. New York: Oxford Univ. Press. (1972).

1013. Woodward, Ralph Lee, Jr. Central America: A Nation Divided. New York: Oxford Univ. Press (1976).

## B. The Redistribution of Wealth, Status and Power

1014. Allman, T. D. Rising to Rebellion. Harper's. March 1981, p. 31.

1015. Barkin, David and Vita R. Manitas. Cuba: The Logic of the Revolution. Andover: Warner Modular (1973).

1016. Becker, David G. The New Bourgeoisie and the Limits of Dependency: Mining, Class and Power in "Revolutionary" Peru. Princeton: Princeton Univ. Press (1983).

1017. Bertugli, David. "Monterrey: Mexico's Industrial El Dorado." 134 Town and Country, 118 (Nov. 1980).

1018. Black, George. Triumph of the People: The Sandinista Revolution in Nicaragua. Westport: Laurence Hill (1981).

1019. Blasier, Cole. The Hovering Giant: U.S. Responses to Revolutionary Change in Latin America. Pittsburgh: Univ. of Pittsburgh Press (1976).

1020. Bledel, Enrique E. The Latin American Development Process and New Legislative Trends. 10 Georgia J. Int'l & Comp. L. 325 (1980).

1021. Boorstein, Edward. Allende's Chile: An Inside View. New York: Int'l. Publishers (1977).

1022. ___________. The Economic Transformation of Cuba. New York: Monthly Review Press (1968).

1023. Borge, Tomás, et. al. Sandinistas Speak. New York: Pathfinder (1982).

1024. Brundenius, Claes. Revolutionary Cuba: The Challenge of Economic Growth with Equity. Boulder: Westview Press (1984).

1025. Bullejos, José. The Reform, Díaz and the Revolution. 13 Americas 11 (No. 7, July 1961).

1026. Cardenal, Ernesto. In Cuba. Trans. Donald D. Walsh. New York: New Directions (1974).

1027. ___________. Hacia el Partido de la Revolución. Managua: Min. del Interior (1980).

1028. Cardoso, Fernando H. and Enzo Faletto. Dependency and Development in Latin America. Trans. Marjory M. Urquidi. Berkeley: U. of Cal. Press (1979).

1029. Castro, Fidel. History Will Absolve Me! New York: Lyle Stuart (1961).

1030. ___________. Selected Speeches. New York: Pathfinder (1982).

1031. ___________. Habla Fidel Castro. Philadelphia: ISHI (1978).

1032. Cavas, Jorge and Selowsky, Marcelo. "Potential Distributive Effects of Naturalization Policies: The Economic Aspects," Income Distribution and Growth in Less-Developed Countries, ed. Charles

R. Frank, Jr. and Richard C. Webb. Washington: The Brookings Institution (1977).

1033. Chace, James. Getting Out of the Central America Maze. The New York Review of Books, June 24, 1982, p. 20.

1034. Che Guevara Speaks: Selected Speeches and Writings. Ed. George Lavan. New York: Pathfinder Press (1967).

1035. Collier, Jane. Law and Social Change in Zinacantan. Stanford: Stanford Univ. Press (1973).

1036. ____________. Political Leadership and Legal Change in Zinacantan. 11 Law & Soc. Rev. 131 (1976).

1037. Cuba económica. Economía y desarrollo, no. 10 (March-April 1972).

1038. "Cuba: La Revolución en Marcha." 2 Latin American Perspectives, no. 4 (Supp. 1975).

1039. Cuba, Santiago. Los Tribunales Populares. 7 Verde olivo, no. 41 (October 16, 1966).

1040. Del Prado, Jorge. Is There a Revolution in Peru? 14 World Marxist Rev. 17 (Jan. 1971).

1041. Domínguez, Jorge. "Revolutionary Values and Development Performance: China, Cuba and the Soviet Union," in Values in Development, ed. Harold Lasswell, Daniel Lerner, and John Montgomery. Cambridge: M.I.T. Press (1977).

1042. ______________. Cuba: Order and Revolution. Cambridge: Harvard Univ. Press (1978).

1043. ________________, ed. Mexico's Political Economy. Beverly Hills: Sage (1982).

1044. Eckstein, Susan. The Impact of Revolution: A Comparative Analysis of Mexico and Bolivia. Beverly Hills: Sage Publications (1976).

1045. ______________. The Poverty of Revolution and the State and Urban Poor in Mexico. Princeton: Princeton Univ. Press (1977).

1046. Epstein, Edward C. Business-Government Relations in Mexico: The Echeverría Challenge to the Existing Development Model. 12 Case Western Res J. Int'l L. 525 (1980).

1047. ________________. Introduction to Recent Developments in Mexican Law: Politics of Modern Nationalism. 4 Denver J. Int'l. L. & Pol. 55 (1974).

1048. Evans, Peter. Dependent Development: The Alliance of Multinational, State, and Local Capital in Brazil. Princeton: Princeton Univ. Press (1979).

1049. Fernández, Florestan. Reflections on the Brazilian Counter-Revolution. Armonk, N.Y.: M. E. Sharpe (1981).

1050. Fidel Castro on Chile. New York: Pathfinder (1982).

1051. Findley, Roger W. Presidential Intervention in the Economy and the Rule of Law in Colombia. 28 Am. J. Comp. L. 423 (1980).

1052. Fitzgerald, Edmund V. K. The State and Economic Development: Peru Since 1968. Cambridge: Cambridge Univ. Press (1976).

1053. Furnish, Dale B. The Hierarchy of Peruvian Laws: Context for Law and Development. 19 Am. J. Comp. L. 91 (1971).

1054. ________________. Law and Development in Peru: Policy-Making for Progress in the Third World. 2 Michigan Academician 3 (1969).

1055. Furtado, Celso. Economic Development in Latin America. 2d ed. Trans. Suzette Macedo. Cambridge: Cambridge Univ. Press (1976).

1056. Gettleman, Marvin E., et al., eds. El Salvador: Central America in the New Cold War. New York: Grove Press (1981).

1057. González Casanova, Pablo. The Economic Development of Mexico. 243 Scientific American 192 (1980).

1058. González Gómez, Andrés. Perú: Acumlación y Crisis en una Economía Dependentista. México: UNAM (1980).

1059. Griffiths, John and Peter Griffiths, eds. Cuba: The Second Decade. London: Writers & Readers Publishing Coop. (1979).

1060. Guevara, Ernesto Che. "Man and Socialism in Cuba," in Man and Socialism in Cuba. Ed. Bertram Silverman. New York: Atheneum (1971).

1061. Hammergren, Linn A. Development and the Process of Administrative Reform. Lessons from Latin America. Boulder: Westview Press (1983).

1062. Hansen, Roger D. The Politics of Mexican Development. Baltimore: Johns Hopkins Univ. Press (1974).

1063. Hanson, Simon G. Utopia in Uruguay, Chapters in the Economic History of Uruguay. New York: Oxford Univ. Press (1938).

1064. Harnecker, Marta, ed. Cuba: Dictatorship or Democracy Westport: Lawrence Hill & Co. (1979).

1065. Huberman, Leo and Paul M. Sweezy. Regis Debray and the Latin American Revolution. New York: Monthly Review Press (1968).

1066. Karst, Kenneth L., Murray L. Schwartz, and Audrey J. Schwartz. The Evolution of Law in the Barrios of Caracas. Los Angeles: UCLA Latin American Center (1973).

1067. Keohane, Robert O. and Joseph S. Nye. Power and Interdependence: World Politics in Transition. Boston: Little, Brown (1977).

1068. Klarén, Peter F. Modernization, Dislocation and Aprismo: Origins of the Peruvian Aprista Party, 1870-1932. Austin: Univ. of Texas Press (1973).

1069. Kozolchyk, Boris. Law and Credit Structure in Latin America. 7 Virginia J. of Int. L. 1 (1967).

1070. ________________. Toward a Theory of Law in Economic Development: The Costa Rican USAID-ROCAP project. 1971 Arizona St. L. J. 681 (1971).

1071. La Feber, Walter. Inevitable Revolution. The Atlantic Monthly, June 1982, p. 74.

1072. Laqueur, Walter, ed. The Guerrilla Reader: A Historical Anthology. New York: New American Library (1977).

1073. López-Valdez, Abelardo. Developing the Role of Law in Social Change: Past Endeavors and Future Opportunities in Latin America and the Caribbean. 7 Lawyer of the Americas 1 (1975).

1074. Loveman, Brian. Chile: The Legacy of Hispanic Capitalism. New York: Oxford Univ. Press (1979).

1075. Lowenthal, Abraham F. Peru's Ambiguous Revolution. 52 Foreign Affairs 799 (1974).

1076. Lowy, Michael. The Politics of Combined and Uneven Development: The Theory of Permanent Revolution. London: Verso (1981).

1077. Malloy, James M., ed. Authoritarianism and Corporatism in Latin America. Pittsburgh: Univ. of Pittsburgh Press (1977).

1078. ________ and Richard S. Thorn, eds. Beyond the Revolution: Bolivia Since 1952. Pittsburgh: Univ. of Pittsburgh Press (1971).

1079. Martz, John D. and David J. Myers. Venezuela: The Democratic Experience. New York: Praeger (1977).

1080. Maynard, Fredelle. Cuba: The Revolutionary Life. 244 The Atlantic Monthly no. 4 (Oct. 1979), p. 4.

1081. Means, Robert A. Underdevelopment and the Develop ment of Law: Corporations and Corporations Law in Nineteenth Century Colombia. Chapel Hill: Univ. of North Carolina Press (1980).

1082. Mesa-Lago, Carmelo. The Economy of Socialist Cuba: A Two-Decade Appraisal. Albuquerque: Univ. of New Mexico Press (1981).

1083. ________________, ed. Revolutionary Change in Cuba. Pittsburgh: Univ. of Pittsburgh Press (1971).

1084. "Mexico in the Eighties." 9 Latin American Perspectives, no. 1 (Winter 1982).

1085. Mexico's Drive to Industrialize." Forbes, Oct. 29, 1979, p. 44.

1086. Migdal, Joel S. Peasants, Politics and Revolution. Princeton: Princeton Univ. Press (1974).

1087. Murphy, E. E., Jr. Decision 24, Mexicanzation, and the New International Economic Order: The Anatomy of Disincentive. 13 Texas Int'l L. J. 289 (1978).

1088. Nicaragua: A People's Revolution. Washington DC: EPICA Task Force (1980).

1089. Novoa, Eduardo. El Derecho como Obstáculo al Cambio Social. México: Siglo XXI (1975).

1090. O'Connor, James. The Origins of Socialism in Cuba. Ithaca: Cornell Univ. Press (1970).

1091. Parry, J. H. and Philip Sherlock. A Short History of the West Indies. 3d ed. New York: St. Martin's Press (1971).

1092. Pendle, George. A History of Latin America. Middlesex: Penguin Books (1980).

1093. Pereira, Luiz Bresser. Development and Crisis in Brazil, 1930-1982. Trans. Marcia Van Dyke. Boulder: Westview Press (1984).

1094. "Peru: Bourgeois Revolution and Class Struggle." 4 Latin American Perspectives, no. 3 (Summer 1977).

1095. Raat, Willam Dirk, ed. Mexico: From Independence to Revolution, 1810-1910. Lincoln: Univ. of Nebraska Press (1982).

1096. Revolutionay Nicaragua. 8 Latin American Perspectives No. 2 (1981).

1097. Reyna, José Luis and Richard S. Weinert. Authoritarianism in Mexico. Philadelphia: ISHI (1977).

1098. Reynolds, Clark. La Economía Mexicana. Su Estructur y Crecimiento en el Siglo XX. México: Fondo de Cultura Económica (1973).

1099. Ritter, Archibald. The Economic Development of Revolutionary Cuba. New York: Praeger (1974).

1100. Roca, Sergio. Cuban Economic Policy and Ideology: The Ten Million Ton Sugar Harvest. Sage Professional Papers in International Studies 4, no. 02-044 (1976).

1101. Ropp, Steven C. and James A. Morris, eds. Central America: Crisis and Adaptation. Albuquerque: Univ. of New Mexico Press (1984).

1102. Rural Class Relations. 9 Latin American Perspectives No. 3 (1982).

1103. Sánchez-Albornoz, Nicolás. The Population of Latin America: A History. Trans. W.A.R. Richardson. Berkeley: Univ. of Cal. Press (1974)

1104. Sanders, Barry A. The New Mexican Industrial Development Plan. 14 International Lawyer 652 1980).

1105. Sandino, Augusto and Carlos Fonseca Amador. Nicaragua: La Estrategia de la Victoria. México: Ed. Nuestro Tiempo (1980).

1106. Scobie, James S. Buenos Aires: Plaza to Suburb, 1870-1910. New York: Oxford Univ. Press (1974).

1107. Stallings, Barbara. Class Conflict and Economic Development in Chile, 1958-1973. Stanford: Stanford Univ. Press (1978).

1108. Stepan, Alfred. Authoritarian Brazil. New Haven: Yale Univ. Press (1973).

1109. ______________. The State and Society: Peru in Comparative Perspective. Princeton: Princeton Univ. Press (1978).

1110. Syrquin, Moshe and Simon Teitel, eds. Trade, Stability, Technology and Equity in Latin America. New York: Academic Press (1982).

1111. Thurber, Clarence E. and Lawrence S. Graham. Development Administration in Latin America. Durham: Duke Univ. Press (1973).

1112. Trubek, David. Law, Planning and the Development of the Brazilian Capital Market: A Study of Law in Economic Change. New York: NYU Institute of Finance, Graduate School of Business Administration, Bulletin nos. 72-73 (1971).

1113. _________. Legal Development and Social Change in Latin America and the Caribbean. 62 A. B. A. J. 484 (1976).

1114. Véliz, Claudio. The Centralist Tradition of Latin America. Princeton: Princeton Univ. Press (1980).

1115. Vylder, Stefan de. Allende's Chile: The Political Economy of the Rise and Fall of the Unidad Popular. Cambridge: Cambridge Univ. Press (1976).

1116. Walker, Thomas V., ed. Nicaragua in Revolution. New York: Praeger (1982).

1117. Weber, Henri. Nicaragua: The Sandinist Revolution. Trans. Patrick Camiller. London: Verso Editions (1981).

1118. Wheelock, Jaime. Diciembre Victorioso. Managua: Senapep (1979).

1119. Wiarda, Howard. Law and Political Development in Latin America: Toward a Framework for Analysis. 19 Am. J. Comp. L. 434 (1971).

1120. _____________, ed. Politics and Social Change in Latin America: The Distinct Tradition. 2d ed. rev. Amherst: Univ. of Massachusetts Press (1982).

1121. _____________. Rift and Revolution: The Central American Imbroglio. Washington: American Enterprise Institute for Public Policy Research (1984).

1122. Womack, John, Jr. El Salvador and the Central American War. 12 Socialist Review, no. 2 (March-April 1982), 9-30.

1123. _____________. Zapata and the Mexican Revolution. New York: Vintage Books (1968).

1124. Wynia, Gary. The Politics of Latin American Development. New York: Cambridge Univ. Press (1978)

1. Ownership and Use of Property

1125. Alvarez Tabío, Fernando. La propiedad Socialista. 11 Rev. Cub. Jur. 11 (1962).

1126. Copyright Protection in the Americas. 4th Ed. Prepared by Bureau of Legal Affairs, OAS General Secretariat. Dobbs Ferry, NY: Oceana (1979).

1127. Merino, Brito. Cambios jurídicos sobre la propiedad en Cuba. 3 Rev. Cub. der., no. 8 (1974), p. 155.

1128. Musto, Nestor J. Derechos Reales. Santa Fe (Argentina): Rubinzal y Culzoni (1981-1983).

1129. Novoa, Eduardo. Los Conceptos de Estado y propiedad en el Derecho Positivo Chileno. 36 Revista De Derecho Económico (1964).

1130. Perea Rosello, P. L. propiedad y Posesión en el Derecho Romano y en el Common Law. Rev. de Der. Puertorriqueño, (1961), p. 7.

1131. Peruvian Social Property Law. 16 Harv. Int'l L. J. 132 (1975).

1132. Private Enterprise. Granma Weekly Review, Oct. 14, 1979, p. 10.

1133. Salaries and Taxes in Cuba. Granma Weekly Review, April 1, 1979, p. 6.

1134. "The Social Function of Property," in Royal Institute of International Affairs, Agrarian Reform in

Latin America, Ed. Thomas L. Smith. New York: Knopf (1962).

a. Allocation of Land and Shelter

1) Ideology and Reality in Agrarian Reform

1136. Acosta, José. Las leyes de reforma agraria en Cuba y el sector privado campesino. Economía y Desarrollo, no. 12 (July-August 1972).

1137. "Agribusiness Targets in Latin America." NACLA Report on the Americas, Vol. 12, no. 1 (Jan.-Feb. 1978).

1138. Aranda, Sergio. La revolución agraria en Cuba. 6th ed. México: Siglo XXI (1975).

1139. Arévalo-Salazar, L. The Legal Insecurity of Rural Property in Colombia: A Case Study of the Notarial and Registry Systems. Univ. of Wisc. Land Tenure Center Res. Paper no. 45 (April 1972).

1140. Bailey, H. M. and F. H. Cruz. The Latin Americans: Past and Present. Boston: Houghton Mifflin (1972).

1141. Barraclough, Solon. Agrarian Structure in Latin America. Lexington: Lexington Books (1973).

1142. Beals, Ralph L. The Peasant Marketing System of Oaxaca, Mexico. Berkeley: Univ. of Cal. Press (1975).

1143. Boorstein, Edward. Allende's Chile: An Inside View. New York: Int'l Publishers (1977).

1144. Burbach, Roger. Nicaragua: The Course of the Revolution. 31 Monthly Rev. 28 (1980).

1145. Centro de Estudios de Derecho y Sociedad. La Jurisprudencia Agraria. Lima: CEDYS (1980).

1146. Chevalier, Francois. Land and Society in Colonial Mexico: The Great Hacienda. Berkeley: Univ. of Cal. Press (1963).

1147. "Chile: Blood on the Peaceful Road." 1 Latin American Perspectives, no. 2 (Summer 1974).

1148. Chonchol, J. "Análisis Crítico de la Reforma Agraria Cubana," in El Trimestre Economics. Vol. XXX (1).

1149. Cleaves, Peter and Martin Scurrah. Agriculture, Bureaucracy and Military Government in Peru. Ithaca: Cornell Univ. Press. (1980).

1150. Collins, Joseph. What Difference Could a Revolution Make? San Francisco: Institute for Food and Development Policy (1982).

1151. Comment. Expropiation and the Venezuelan Law of Agrarian Reform. 6 Columbia J. Trans. L. 273 (1967).

1152. Dorner, Peter, ed. Land Reform in Latin America. Madison: Land Economics (1970).

1153. Doughty, Paul L. Huaylas: An Andean District in Search of Progress. Ithaca: Cornell Univ. Press (1968)

1154. Duff, Ernest A. Agrarian Reform in Colombia. New York: Praeger (1968).

1155. Ellsworth, D. Mexico Opens the Door to Resort Development. 5 Real Estate Rev. 36 (1975).

1156. El Salvador: Background to the Crisis. Cambridge: Central America Information Office (1982).

1157. Farley, Rawle. "Agrarian Reform: Legal Response to a Major Social Issue," in The Economics of Latin America. New York: Harper and Row (1972).

1158. Feder, E. The Rape of the Peasantry: Latin America's Land Holding System. Garden City: Doubleday (1971).

1159. Findley, Roger. Ten Years of Land Reform in Colombia. 1972 Wisc. L. Rev. 686 (1972).

1160. Flores, Edmundo. "The Economics of Land Reform." 92 International Labor Review no. 1 (July 1965), 30.

1161. ________. Land Reform and the Alliance for Progress. Princeton: Center of Int'l Studies (1963).

1162. Franco, J. M. The Legal Insecurity of Landed Property in Venezuela: A Case Study of the Registry System. 3 Lawyer of the Americas 464 (1971).

1163. Frundi, T. Henry. Fat Latin Profits for U.S. Agribusiness. 34 Bus. & Society Rev. 15 (Summer 1980).

1164. García, Antonio. El Nuevo Problema Agrario de la América Latina. México: UNAM (1981).

1165. Gettleman, Marvin E., et al., eds. El Salvador: Central America in the New Cold War. New York: Grove Press (1981).

1166. Griffiths, John and Peter, eds. Cuba: The Second Decade. London: Writers and Readers Pub. Co-Op. (1979).

1167. Grindle, Merilee S. Official Interpretations of Rural Underdevelopment: Mexico in the 1970's. Working Papers in U.S.-Mexican Studies #2. Los Angeles: UCLA (1981).

1168. ______________. Whatever Happened to Agrarian Reform? The Latin American Experience. Technical Papers Series No. 23, University of Texas at Austin, Institute of Latin American Studies (1980).

1169. Gros-Espiell, Héctor. The Right of Development as a Human Right. 16 Tex. J. Int'l L. 189 (1981).

1170. Gutelman, Michel. L'Agriculture Socialisée à Cuba. Paris: F. Maspero (1967).

1171. Halperin, Rhoda and James Dow, eds. Peasant Livelihood: Studies in Economic Anthropology and Cultural Ecology. New York: St. Martin's Press (1977).

1172. Harper, George R. Cuban and Peruvian Agrarian Reforms: At the Crossroads. 24 U. Miami L. Rev. 763 (1970).

1173. Harris, Charles H. III. A Mexican Family Empire: The Latifundio of the Sánchez Navarros, 1765-1867. Austin: Univ. of Texas Press (1975).

1174. Huizer, G. Peasant Rebellion in Latin America. Harmondsworth: Penguin (1973).

1175. Hurtado-Edwards, J.L. and Smith, R.G. The Chilean Agrarian Reform. 6 Inter-Am. L. Rev. 93 (1964).

1176. Janvry, Alain de. The Agrarian Question & Reformism in Latin America. Baltimore: John Hopkins Univ. Press (1981).

1177. Karst, Kenneth. The Colombian Land Reform: The Contribution of an Independent Judiciary. 14 Am. J. Comp. L. 118 (1965).

1178. ______________, and N. C. Clement. Legal Institutions and Development: Lessons from the Mexican Ejido. 16 UCLA L. Rev. 281 (1969).

1179. Kaufman, Robert R. The Politics of Land Reform in Chile, 1950-1970. Cambridge: Harvard Univ. Press (1972).

1180. Land and the Forest-Dwelling South American Indian: The Role of National Law. 27 Buffalo L. Review. 759 (1981).

1181. Landsberger, Henry A., ed. Latin American Peasant Movements. Ithaca: Cornell Univ. Press (1969)

1182. Lehmann, D., ed. Agrarian Reform and Agrarian Reformism: Studies of Peru, Chile, China and India. London: Faber (1974).

1183. Le Riverend, J. "Conclusiones Sobre la Reforma Agraria Cubana" in Les Problemes Agraires des Ameriques Latines 653 (1967).

1184. Lockhart, James. "E comienda and Hacienda: The Evolution of the Great Estate in the Spanish Indies." 49 HAHR 411 (1969).

1185. López Michelsen, A. "Hacia una verdadera reforma que complete la Revolución en Marcha," in Tierra: 10 Ensayos Sobre la Reforma Agraria en Colombia 85 (1961).

1186. Marco Juridico De La Reforma Agraria Nicaraguense. Direccion General de la Reforma Agraria. Ministeri de Desarrollo Agropecuario y Reforma Agraria. Managua (1982).

1187. McBride, George M. Chile: Land and Society. New York: American Geographical Society (1936).

1188. ____________. The Land Systems of Mexico. New York: American Geographical Society (1923).

1189. McClintock, Cynthia. Peasant Cooperatives and Political Change in Peru. Princeton: Princeton Univ. Press (1981).

1190. Meek, M. Land Transfer and Finance in Latin America. 4 Denver J. Int'l L. & Pol. 25 (1974).

1191. Mexican Agrarian Rights: Who Do They Benefit? 8 Calif. West Int'l L. J. 130 (1978).

1192. Migdal, Joel S. Peasants, Politics and Revolution. Princeton: Princeton Univ. Press (1974).

1193. Moberg, David and John Echeverri-Sent. El Salvador 'Reform' is a Shell Game. In These Times (March 18-31, 1981).

1194. Paige, Jeffery M. Agrarian Revolution. New York: Free Press (1975).

1195. Pásara, Luis. Reforma Agraria: Derecho y Conflicto. Lima: Instituto de Estudios Peruanos (1978).

1196. Pearse, Andrew. The Latin American Peasant. London: Frank Cass (1975).

1197. "Peru: Bourgeois Revolution and Class Struggle." 4 Latin American Perspectives, no. 3 (Summer, 1977).

1198. Prosterman, Roy L. "Land Reform in Latin America: How to Have a Revolution Without a Revolution." 42 Wash. L. Rev. 189 (1966).

1199. ________________. The Unmaking of a Land Reform. The New Republic, Aug. 9, 1982, p. 21.

1200. ________________, Jeffrey M. Riedinger, Mary N. Temple. Land Reform in El Salvador: The Democratic Alternative. 144 World Affairs 36 (Summer 1981).

1201. Revolutionary Nicaragua. 8 Latin American Perspectives no. 2 (Spring 1981).

1202. Reyna, José Luis and Richard S. Weinert, eds. Authoritarianism in Mexico. Philadelphia: ISHI (1977).

1203. Rosenn, Keith S. Comment, Puerto Rican Land Reform: The History of an Instructive Experiment. 73 Yale L. J. 334 (1963).

1204. Rowles, James P. Law and Agrarian Reform in Costa Rica: The Legislative Phase. 14 Lawyer of the Americas 149 (1982)

1205. Santistevan, J. La Huelga en el Perú. Historia y Derecho. Lima: CEDYS (1981).

1206. Scobie, James. Revolution on the Pampas: A Social History of Argentine Wheat, 1860-1910. Austin: Inst. of Latin American Studies, Univ. of Texas (1964).

1207. Simon, Laurence and James Stephens, Jr. El Salvador Land Reform 1980-1981: Impact Audit. Boston: Oxfam-America (1981).

1208. Smith, T. Lynn. Los impedimentos a la reforma agraria en la América Latina. 19 Problemas Internacionales 23 (1972).

1209. "The Social Function of Property," in Royal Institute of International Affairs, Agrarian Reform in Latin America, Ed. Thomas L. Smith. New York: Knopf (1965).

1210. Stavenhagen, Rodolfo, ed. Agrarian Problems and Peasant Movements in Latin America. Garden City: Doubleday (1970).

1211. Steenland, Kyle. Agrarian Reform Under Allende: Peasant Revolt in the South. Albuquerque: Univ. of New Mexico Press (1977).

1212. Tena-Ramírez, Felipe. Leyes Fundamentales de México, 1808-1982. 11th ed. rev. México: Editorial Porrúa (1982).

1213. Thome, Joseph R. The Colombian Agrarian Reform: Legal Limitations on the Process of Expropriation. 8 Inter-Am. L. Rev. 269 (1966).

1214. ___________________. Expropriation in Chile under the Frei Agrarian Reform. 19 Am. J. Comp. L. 489 (1971).

1215. _______________. The Process of Land Reform in Latin America. 1968 Wisc. L. Rev. 6 (1968).

1216. Trazegnies, Fernando de. El Caso Huayanay: El Derecho en Situación-Límite. Cuadernos Agrarios, I (1977), p. 73 and II (1978) p. 47. (Lima: Instituto Peruano de Derecho Agrario).

1217. Warriner, D. Land Reform in Principle and Practice. Oxford: Clarendon Press (1969).

1218. Wheelock, J. "Nicaragua's Plans for Agriculture," in The Nicaraguan Revolution, eds. Pedro Camejo and Fred Murphy. New York: Pathfinder Press (1979).

1219. Whetten, N. Rural Mexico. Chicago: Univ. of Chicago Press (1948).

1220. Wilkie, James W. Measuring Land Reform. Los Angeles: Latin American Center, UCLA (1974).

1221. Williams, S. Popular Capitalism: A Selective Route to Agricultural Development. 3 Int'l. Rel. 457 (1969).

1222. Womack, John, Jr. Zapata and the Mexican Revolution New York: Knopf (1969).

2) Urban Migrations and the Law of Housing

1223. Acosta, Maruja and Jorge Hardoy. Urban Reform in Revolutionary Cuba. New Haven: Yale University, Antilles Research Program (1973).

1224. Arias de Blois, Jorge. La población de Centro-América y sus perspectivas. Guatemala: Univ. de San Carlos (1966).

1225. Beyer, Glenn H., ed. The Urban Explosion in Latin America. Ithaca: Cornell Univ. Press (1967).

1226. Burke, T.R. Law and Development: Chilean Housing Program. 2 Lawyer of the Americas 173 (1969).

1227. Butterworth, D. and J.K. Chance. Latin American Urbanization. Cambridge: Cambridge Univ. Press (1981).

1228. Colina. The Housing Situation in Cuba. Granma Weekly Review., April 16, 1978, at 6, col. 1.

1229. Cornelius, Wayne. "The Political Sociology of Cityward Migration in Latin America: Toward Empirical Theory," in F. Rabinowitz and F. Trueblood, eds., I Latin American Urban Research 95 (1971).

1230. Dietz, Henry. Urban Squatter Settlements in Peru: A Case History and Analysis. 11 J. Inter. Am. Development 353 (1969).

1231. Doebele, W.A. Private Market & Low Income Urbanization: The Private Market Subdivisions of Bogotá. 25 Am. J. Comp. L. 531 (1977).

1232. Garza, Gustavo and Marta Scheingart. Mexico City: The Emerging Megalopolis. 6 Latin Am. Res. Rev. 81 (1978).

1233. Hardoy, Jorge, ed. Urbanization in Latin America: Approaches and Issues. Garden City: Anchor Books (1975).

1234. Harris, W.D., Jr. The Growth of Latin American Cities. Athens, Ohio: Ohio Univ. Press (1971).

1235. Jesús, Carolina M. de. Child of the Dark. New York: New American Library (1962).

1236. Karst, Kenneth, L. Rights in Land & Housing in an Informal Legal System: The Barrios of Caracas. 19 Am. J. Comp. L. 550 (1971).

1237. Karst, Kenneth, Murray Schwartz, and Audrey J. Schwartz. The Evolution of Law in the Barrios of

Caracas. Los Angeles: UCLA Latin America Center (1973).

1238. Kaufman, C. Urbanization, Material Satisfaction, and Mass Political Involvement: The Poor in Mexico City. 4 Comp. Pol. Studies 2 (1971).

1239. Lloyd, P. The "Young Towns" of Lima: Aspects of Urbanization in Peru. Cambridge: Cambridge Univ. Press (1980).

1240. Manaster, K. The Problem of Urban Squatters in Developing Countries: Peru. 1968 Wisconsin L. Rev. 23 (1968).

1241. Mangin, William. Latin American Squatter Settlement: A Problem and a Solution. 2 Latin American Res. Rev. 65 (1967).

1242. Morse, Richard M. Recent Research on Latin Americar Urbanization: A Selective Survey with Commentary. 1 Latin American Res. Rev. 35 (1963).

1243. Nash, Manning. Machine Age Maya. Chicago: Univ. c Chicago Press (1967).

1244. Pérez Perdomo, Rogelio and Pedro Inikken. Law and Housing Ownership in the Barrios of Caracas. 3 Urban L. & Pol. 365 (1980).

1245. Perlman, Janice E. The Myth of Marginality: Urban Poverty and Politics in Rio de Janeiro. Berkeley: Univ. of Cal. Press (1976).

1246. Ray, T. The Politics of the Barrios of Caracas. Berkeley: Univ. of Cal. Press (1969).

1247. Roberts, Bryan. Cities of Peasants: The Political Economy of Urbanization in the Third World. Beverly Hills: Sage Publications (1978).

1248. ______________. Organizing Strangers. Austin: Uni of Tex. Press (1973).

1249. Robinson, H. Secondary Markets for Home Mortgages: Latin American and Caribbean Experience: 10 J. Int'l L. & Econ. 89 (1975).

1250. Rosenn, Keith. Controlled Rents and Uncontrolled Inflation: The Brazilian Dilemma. 17 Am. J. Comp. I 239 (1 969).

1251. Ruiz Massieu, José F. Derecho Urbanístico. México: UNAM (1981).

1252. Sánchez-Albornoz, Nicolás. The Population of Latin America. Trans. W.A.R. Richardson. Berkeley: Univ. of Cal. Press (1974).

1253. Shirley, Robert W. "Legal Institutions and Early Industrial Growth," in John Wirth, ed., Manchester and Sao Paulo: Problems of Urban Growth. Stanford: Stanford Univ. Press (1978).

1254. Stearns, Fredric. Urbanization and Public Services. 10 Georgia J. Int'l & Comp. L. 495 (1980).

1255. Symposium: Legal Issues and Urbanization in Developing Countries. 10 Georgia J. Int'l L. 491 (1980).

1256. Tocups, Nora M. City Growth and Cooperation Along the United States/Mexican Border. 10 Ga. J. Int'l L. 619 (1980).

1257. Turack, Daniel C. Freedom of Movement in the Caribbean Community. 11 Denver J. Int'l L. & Pol. 37 (1981).

1258. Turner, Joseph F. Housing by People. London: Marion Boyars (1976).

1259. Vaughn, D. and W. Feindt. Initial Settlement and Intracity Movement of Migrants in Monterrey, Mexico. 39 J. Am. Inst. Planners 388 (1973).

1260. Wirth, John, ed. Manchester and Sao Paulo: Problems of Urban Growth. Stanford: Stanford Univ. Press (1978).

## b. Organization and Control of Economic Activity

### 1) Rules Governing Commercial Transactions

1261. Aztiria, Enrique. Commercial Law and Private Law in Countries Having a Continental Legal System. 1 Inter-Am. L. Rev. 123 (1959).

1262. Barrera Graf, Jorge. El Derecho Mercantil en la América latina. México: UNAM (1963).

1263. Boorstein, Edward. Allende's Chile: An Inside View. New York: Int'l Publishers (1977).

1264. Cerruti-Aicardi, Héctor J. The Performance of Contractual Obligations. 3 Inter-Am. L. Rev. 95 (1961).

1265. Clagett, Helen L. Sources of the Commercial Law of Mexico. 18 Tulane L. Rev. 437 (1944).

1266. Cueto-Rúa, Julio. Administrative, Civil and Commercial Contracts in Latin America. 26 Fordham L. Rev. 15 (1957).

1267. Kozolchyk, Boris. Commercial Law Recodification and Economic Development in Latin America. 4 Lawyer of the Americas 189 (1971).

1268. ________. Fairness in Anglo & Latin American Commercial Adjudication. 2 Boston Coll. Int'l & Comp. L. Rev. 219 (1979).

1269. ________. Law and the Credit Structure in Latin America. Santa Monica: Rand Corp. (1966). Also, 7 VA. J. Int'l L. 1 (1967).

1270. Martz, John D. and David J. Myers. Venezuela: The Democratic Experience. New York: Praeger (1977).

1271. Means, Robert C. Mexican Commercial Law, 1854-1884. 2 Boston Coll. Int'l & Comp. L. Rev. 299 (1978).

1272. Morales-Hernández, A. The 1970 Amendment to the Venezuelan Commercial Banking Law. 3 Lawyer of the Americas 231 (1970).

1273. Norberg, C.R. Inter-American Commercial Arbitration. 1 Lawyer of the Americas 25 (1968).

1274. ________. Inter-American Commercial Arbitration Revisited. 7 Lawyer of the Americas. 275 (1974).

1275. Obregon, Esquivel et al. Latin American Commercial Law. New York: Banks Publishing Co. (1921).

1276. Olavarría Avila, Julio. Los Códigos de Comercio latinoamericanos. Santiago (1961).

1277. Pillado-Salas, Ricardo. Comparative Study of Conditional Sales and Sales where Payment is by Installments. 2 Inter-Am. L. Rev. 145 (1960).

1278. Radway, Robert J. Negotiating in the Caribbean Basin: Trade & Investment Contracts. 4 Int'l Trade L. J. 164 (1978).

1279. Register, L.B. The Dual System of Civil and Commercial Law. 61 U. Pa. L. Rev. 240 (1912).

1280. Rosenn, Keith S. Law and Inflation. Philadelphia: Univ. of Penn. Press (1982).

1281. Shelton, D. "The Banking System: Money and the Goal of Growth," in Ray Vernon, ed., Public Policy and Private Enterprise in Mexico. Cambridge: Harvard U. Press (1964), p. 111.

1282. Stairs, Stanley T., ed. Current Legal Aspects of Doing Business in Latin America. Chicago: ABA Section on Int'l Law and Practice (1981).

1283. Symposium. Latin American Commercial Law. 2 Boston Col. Int'l &. Comp. L. Rev. 215 (1979).

2) Limitations on the Structure and Functioning of Corporate Enterprise

1284. Angulo, Manuel R. Comments on the Status of Foreign Business Corporations Under the Commercial Codes of Argentina and Venezuela. 4 Inter-Am. L. Rev. 159 (1962).

1285. Araujo Cintra, A.C. de. Investors' Remedies Under the New Brazilian Corporation Act. 9 Lawyer of the Americas 531 (1977).

1286. Barnhill, C. Mexican Business Associations. 4 Texas Int'l L. F. 79 (1968).

1287. Carvalhosa, M. Brazilian Experience with Respect to Tender Offers. 3 J. Comp. Corporate L. and Securities Reg. 103 (July 1981).

1288. Collier, David and Ruth Berins Collier. "Who Does What, To Whom, and How: Toward a Comparative Analysis of Latin American Corporations in Latin America," in James M. Malloy, ed., Authoritarianism and Corporatism. Pittsburgh: Univ. of Pittsburgh Press (1977).

1289. Comment, The Peruvian General Law of Industries. 12 Harv. Int'l L. J. 313 (1971).

1290. Crawford, H.P. Capital Structure of a Mexican Corporation. 28 Tulane L. Rev. 45 (1953).

1291. Dillenbeck, R.R. Shareholder's Suits in Mexican Law. 9 Am. J. Comp. L. 78 (1960).

1292. Epstein, Edward C. Business-Government Relations in Mexico: The Echeverria Challenge to the Existing Development Model. 12 Case Western Res. J. Int'l L. 525 (1980).

1293. Furnish, Dale. Chilean Antitrust Law. 19 Am. J. Comp. L. 464 (1971).

1294. Germán, Rafael. Latin American Antitrust. 14 Lawyer of the Americas 1 (1982).

1295. Gladstone, Philip. Theory and Operation of Partnerships Under the Latin American Codes. 16 Tulane L. Rev. 27 (1941).

1296. Gómez, H. The Law of Latin American Business Associations: A Survey. 14 S.W.U.L. Rev. 169 (1960).

1297. Halperín, Julio. Sociedades de responsabilidad limitada. 3d. ed. Buenos Aires (1956).

1298. Haro, R. A Brief Comparison of the Law of Business Organizations in the United States and Mexico. 7 Am. Bus. L. J. 225 (1970).

1299. Horvath, P.A. The Organization and Functions of the Board of Directors of Corporations in Argentina and the U.S. 1 Lawyer of the Americas 1 (1968).

1300. Johnson, Lawrence. An Analysis of the Venezuelan Securities Legislation: Part 1 - The Primary Markets, Part II - The Secondary Markets. 12 Int'l Lawyer 171, 241 (1978).

1301. Jorgensen, Edward. The Peruvian Social Property Law. 16 Harv. Int'l. L. J. 132 (1975).

1302. Juncadella, S. Legislation on Antimonopoly and Unfair Competition: Central America and Panama. 8 Lawyer of the Americas 60 (1976).

1303. Karst, Kenneth, Murray Schwartz, and Audrey J. Schwartz. The Evolution of Law in the Barrios of Caracas. Los Angeles: UCLA Latin American Center (1973).

1304. Kozolchyk, Boris. Toward a Theory on Law in Economic Development: The Costa Rican USAID--ROCAP Law Reform Project. 1971 L. & Soc. Order 681 (1971).

1305. Means, Robert C. Underdevelopment and the Development of Law: Corporations and Corporations Law in 19th Century Colombia. Chapel Hill: Univ. of North Carolina Press (1980).

1306. Skola, Thomas J. An Update on Brazilian Trading Companies and Export Credit. 13 Lawyer of the Americas 421 (1981).

1307. Trubek, David. Law, Planning and the Development of the Brazilian Capital Market: A Study of Law in Economic Change. New York: NYU Institute of

Finance, Graduate School of Business Administration, Bulletin Nos. 72-73 (1971).

3) The Rights (and Wrongs) of Workers

1308. Alba, V. Politics and the Labor Movement in Latin America. Stanford: Stanford Univ. Press (1968).

1309. Alexander, Robert. Labor Relations in Argentina, Brazil and Chile. New York: McGraw Hill (1962).

1310. Análisis del Plan Laboral. Documento de Trabajo Vicaria Pastoral Obrera, No. 7, Santiago de Chile (1979).

1311. Arias Sanchez, Oscar. Grupos de Presion en Costa Rica. 5th ed. San José: Editorial Costa Rica (1980).

1312. Barajas, Santiago. Derecho del Trabajo. México: UNAM (1981)

1313. Barbagelata, Héctor H. Introduction Aux Institutions du Droit du Travail en Amerique Latine. Louvain: Presses Universitaires (1980).

1314. Barrera, Manuel. El Conflicto Obrero en el Enclave Cuprífero Chileno. 40 Revista Mexicana de Sociología, No. 2 (Abril-Junio 1978), p. 613.

1315. Barrera, Manuel. Participation by Occupational Organizations in Economic and Social Planning in Chile. 96 Int'l Lab. Rev. 151 (1967).

1316. Barrios de Chungara, Domitila. Let Me Speak! Trans. Victora Orty. New York: Monthly Review Press (1978).

1317. Biaggi Rodríguez. Las Communidades Laborales en el Perú. 62 Revista del Foro (No. 3/4) 9 (1975).

1318. Blejer, Mario. Strike Activity and Wage Determination under Rapid Inflation: The Chilean Case. 34 Indus. & Lab. Rel. Rev. 356 (1981).

1319. Blum, A. and M. Thompson. Unions and White Collar Workers in Mexico. 26 Indus. & Lab. Rel. Rev. 646 (1972).

1320. Bronstein, A.S. Collective Bargaining in Latin America: Problems & Trends. 117 Int'l Lab. Rev. 583 (1978).

1321. Camacho, Manuel. Control sobre el movimiento obrero en México. 16 Foro internacional, No. 4 (Abril-Junio 1976), p. 496.

1322. Chaudhary, R.L. The Law of Strikes and Picketing in CARICOM Countries. 6 Lawyer of the Americas 710 (1974).

1323. ______________, and G.C. Reid. An Appraisal of the Jamaica Labor Relations and Disputes Act. 8 Lawyer of the Americas 36 (1976).

1324. Clark, Marjorie R. La Organización Obrera en México. México: Ed. ERA (1981).

1325. Cohen, A. Societal Structure Agrarian Reform, and Economic Development in Peru. 18 Inter-American Economic Affairs (1964), p. 45-59.

1326. Coquijo Costa, Carlos. Arbitration of Justice in Labour Law, Brazil. (National Report) In International Society of Labour Law & Social Security, 9th Int'l Congress, Munich, 1978, Reports & Procedures, Vol. 2, p. 26-43 (1978).

1327. Córdova, Efrén. Prospects for Harmonizing Latin American Labour Law. 112 Int'l Lab. Rev. 291 (1975)

1328. Córdova, Efrén, Geraldo Von Potobsky, Jorge Acuña and Antonio Vázques. The Settlement of Labor Disputes in Chile. 103 Int'l Lab. Rev. 333 (1971).

1329. "Cuba: La Revolución en Marcha." 2 Latin American Perspectives, No. 4 (Supp. 1975).

1330. Cuban Economic Research Project. Codification of Labor Law in Latin America, Cuba: A Case Study. Coral Gables: Univ. of Miami (1965).

1331. Davis, Stanley M. and Louis W. Goodman. Workers and Managers in Latin America. Lexington: D.C. Heath (1972).

1332. Dawson, Frank Griffith. Labour Legislation & Social Integration in Guatemala: 1871-1944. 14 Am. J. Comp. L. 124 (1965).

1333. Dias de Silva, A.F. Immunity of Foreign States in Brazilian Labor Courts. 3 Lawyer of the Americas 269 (1971).

1334. Decker, David R. and Ignacio Duran. The Political Economic and Labor Climate in Colombia. Philadelphia: Industrial Research Unit, the Wharten School, Univ. of Penn. (1982).

1335. Epstein, E. Politicization and Income Redistribution in Argentina: The Case of the Peronist Worker. 23 Economic Development and Cultural Change (July 1975).

1336. Espinoza, Juan G., and Andrew S. Zimbalist. Economic Democracy: Workers' Participation in Chilean Industry. New York: Academic Press (1978).

1337. Farfán Sáenz. El Fuero Privativo de Comunidades Laborales. 35 Rev. de Jurisprudencia Peruana 466 (1976).

1338. Febres-Cordero, Carlos. A Look at the Scope of Venezuelan Labor Legislation. 5 Inter-Am. L. Rev. 383 (1963).

1339. Galardy. Work in a socialist society: an honor and a source of creation. Granma Weekley Rev. Oct. 31, 1976, p. 10.

1340. Gladstone, Alan & Oki Muneto. Trade Union Recognition for Collective Bargaining Purposes. 112 Int'l Lab. Rev. 163 (1975).

1341. Gros Espiell, Héctor. La Organizacion Internacional del Trabajo y los Derechos Humanos en la América Latina. Serie G. Estudios doctrinales - UNAM, Instituto de Investigaciones Jurídicas, No. 23. México: UNAM (1978).

1342. Harnecker, Marta, ed. Cuba: Dictatorship or Democracy? Westport: Lawrence Hill & Co. (1979).

1343. Ietswaart, Heleen F.P. Labor Relations Litigation: Chile 1970-1972. 16 Law & Soc'y Rev. 625 (1982).

1344. Jelin, Elizabeth. Conflictos laborales en la Argentina, 1973-1976. 40 Revista Mexicana de Sociología, No. 2 (Abril-Junio 1978), p. 421.

1345. Jenks, Clarence W. La Organización Internacional del Trabajo y la protección de los Derechos Humanos de América. Buenos Aires (1962).

1346. Jorgensen, Edward. The Peruvian Social Property Law. 16 Harv. Int'l L. J. 132 (1975).

1347. Kennedy, Ian M. Cuba's Ley Contra Vagancia - The Law on Loafing. 20 U.C.L.A. L. Rev. 1177 (1973).

1348. Lauterbach, A. Aspects of Industrial Relations in Latin America: Executive Training and Productivity. 17 Ind. & Lab. Rel. Rev. 357 (1964).

1349. Lowenthal, Abraham, ed. The Peruvian Experiment. Princeton: Princeton Univ. Press (1975).

1350. Magill, J. Labor Unions and Political Socialization: A Case Study of Bolivian Workers. New York: Praeger (1974).

1351. Malloy, James M., ed. Authoritarianism and Corporatism in Latin America. Pittsburgh: Univ. Of Pittsburgh Press (1977).

1352. Martz, John D. and David J. Myers. Venezuela: The Democratic Experience. New York: Praeger (1977).

1353. Mesa-Lago, Carmelo. Economic Significance of Unpaid Labor in Socialist Cuba. 22 Ind. & Lab. Rel. Rev. 339 (1968).

1354. Murg, Gary E., and J.C. Fox. Labor Relations Laws: Canada, Mexico, and Western Europe. New York: Practicing Law Institute (1978).

1355. Nash, June. We Eat The Mines and the Mines Eat Us: Dependency and Exploitation in Bolivian Tin Mines. New York: Columbia Univ. Press (1979).

1356. Nash, June, Juan Corradi, and H.A. Spalding, eds. Ideology and Social Change in Latin America. New York: Gordon and Breach (1977).

1357. Okpaluba, C. Freedom of Association in West Indian Labor Law. 7 Lawyer of the Americas 291 (1975).

1358. ____________. The New Regime of Labour Relations Crimes in Trinidad and Tobego. 9 Lawyer of the Americas 79 (1977).

1359. Oligarchy and Democracy in Mexican Unions. 30 Industrial and Labor Relations Review. 207 (1977).

1360. Payne, James L. Labor and Politics in Peru: The System of Political Bargaining. New Haven: Yale Univ. Press (1965).

1361. Pearson. The Communidad Industrial: Peru's Experiment in Worker Management. 27 Inter-Am. Econ. Affairs 15 (1973).

1362. Pérez-Stable, Marifeli. Institutionalization and Worker's Response. 6 Cuban Studies, No. 2 (July 1976).

1363. Pérez Pino and Pérez Fernández de Cossío. El Accidente del Trabajo en la Legislación Cubana. 2 Rev. Cub. Der., No. 6 (1973), p. 159.

1364. Poblete-Troncoso, Moisés and Burnett, Ben G. The Rise of the Latin American Labor Movement. New Haven: College & Univ. Press (1960).

1365. Price, Waterhouse & Co. Doing Business in Brazil (1980).

1366. ______________. Doing Business in Colombia (1978).

1367. ______________. Doing Business in Venezuela (1975), (1981).

1368. ______________. Doing Business in Mexico (1979), (1981).

1369. ______________. Doing Business in Chile (1979).

1370. ______________. Doing Business in Argentina (1980).

1371. Revolutionary Nicaragua. 8 Latin American Perspectives, No. 2 (Spring 1981).

1372. Roemer, H. Development of Medical Services under Social Security in Latin America. 108 Int'l Lab. Rev. 1 (1973).

1373. Sandoval, J. The New Mexican Federal Labor Law: An Analysis. Part I: 2 Lawyer of the Americas 386 (1970); Part II: 3 Lawyer of the Americas 11 (1971).

1374. Santistevan, J. La Huelga en el Perú. Historia y Derecho. Lima: CEDYS (1980).

1375. The Settlement of Labor Disputes in Mexico. 103 Int'l Lab. Rev. 477 (1971).

1376. Spalding, Hobart A., Jr. Organized Labor in Latin America: Historical Case Studies of Urban Workers in Dependent Societies. New York: Harper and Row (1977).

1377. U.S. Bureau of Labor Statistics. Labor Law and Practice in Argentina. Washington: U.S.G.P.O. (1968).

1378. Urrutia-Montoya, Miguel. The Development of the Colombian Labor Movement. New Haven: Yale Univ. Press (1969).

1379. Woodward, Ralph Lee. Urban Labor and Communism in Cuba. 3 Caribbean Studies, No. 3 (October 1963).

1380. "Workers and Unions." 4 Cuba Review No. 1 (1974).

1381. Zapata, Francisco. The Chilean Labor Movement under Salvador Allende 1970-1973. 8 Latin American Perspectives 85 (1976).

1382. Zeitlin, M. Revolutionary Politics and the Cuban Working Class. Princeton: Princeton Univ. Press (1967).

1383. Ziskind, David. Reflections on Constitutional Labor Law. 2 Comp. Lab. L. 69 (1977).

4) Remedies of Consumers for the Mischief of Producers

1384. Bledel, E. Food Regulation in Latin America. 28 Food, Drug & Cosm. L. J. 585 (1973).

5) Treatment of the Dispossessed

1385. Cardoso de Oliveira, Moacyr Velloso. Social Security in Brazil. 84 Int'l Lab. Rev. 376 (1961).

1386. Carrillo Prieto, Ignacio. Derecho de la Seguridad Social. México: UNAM (1981).

1387. Díaz-Briqnets, Sergio. The Health Revolution in Cuba. Austin: Univ. of Texas Press (1983).

1388. Kaufman, C. Urbanization, Material Satisfaction, and Mass Political Involvement: The Poor in Mexico City. 4 Comp. Pol. Studies 2 (1971).

1389. Malloy, James M. The Politics of Social Security in Brazil. Pittsburgh: Univ. of Pittsburgh Press (1979).

1390. Mesa-Lago, Carmelo. Social Security in Latin Ameri Pittsburgh: Univ. of Pittsburgh Press (1978).

1391. Roemer, H. Development of Medical Services under Social Security in Latin America. 108 Int'l. Lab. Rev. 1 (1973).

1392. ________. Health Development and Political Policy: The Lesson of Cuba. 4 J. Health Pol. & L. 570 (1980).

c. Restrictions on the Process of Personal Accumulation

1) Taxation of Income

1393. Andersen & Co. Tax and Trade Guide. Colombia. 2d ed. Chicago (1972).

1394. Bird, Richard M. and Oliver Oldman, Eds. Readings on Taxation in Developing Countries. Baltimore: Johns Hopkins Univ. Press. 3d ed. (1975).

1395. Evans, John S. The Evolution of The Mexican Tax System Since 1970. Technical Papers Series No. 34, Univ. of Texas at Austin, Institute of Latin American Studies (1982).

1396. LaVega-Miller, R. Mexican Taxation: Law and Practice. 4 Denver J. Int'l L & Pol. 79 (1974).

1397. Leacock, S. J. Public Utility Regulation in a Developing Country. 8 Lawyer of the Americas 338 (1975).

1398. Martí, Mary. Nicaragua Tax Update. 12 Lawyer of the Americas 661 (1980).

1399. ___________. Survey of Changing Attitudes in Latin American Tax Policy. 8 Int'l Tax J. 115 (1981).

1400. Miller. Mexican Taxation: Law and Practice. 4 Denver J. Int'l. L. & Pol. 79 (1974).

1401. Musgrave, Richard A. Fiscal Reform in Bolivia. Cambridge: Harvard Law School (1981).

1402. Oldman, Oliver. Tax Reform in El Salvador. 6 Inter-Am. L. Rev. 379 (1964).

1403. Rosenn, Keith. Adaptations of the Brazilian Income Tax to Inflation. 21 Stan. L. Rev. 58 (1968).

1404. _________. Law and Inflation. Philadelphia: Univ. of Penn. Press (1982).

1405. _________. Adjusting Taxation of Business Income for Inflation: Lessons from Brazil and Chile. 13 Texas Int'l L. J. 165 (1978).

2) Limitations on the Transfer of Capital

1406. Batiza, Rodolfo. The Evolution of the Fideicomiso (Trust) Concept under Mexican Law. 1 Miami L.Q. 478 (1957).

1407. ______________. El Fideicomiso: Teoría y Práctica México: Edit. Porrúa (1958).

1408. ______________. "Trusts in Mexico," in A. Yiannopoulos, ed., Civil Law in the Modern World. Baton Rouge: Louisiana State Univ. Press (1965), p. 128.

1409. Breithaupt, James F.. Succession in Mexico. 16 Syracuse L. Rev. 622 (1965).

1410. Brutau, J. Puig. An Introduction to the Law of Succession Mortis Causa. 1 Inter-Am. L. Rev. 291 (1959).

1411. Forde, N. M. Family Inheritance, Provisions in the Barbados Succession Act: Redefining the Family. 9 Lawyer of the Americas 115 (1977).

1412. Goldschmidt, Roberto. The Trust in the Countries of Latin America. 3 Inter-Am. L. Rev. 29 (1961).

d. Regulation of Natural Resources

1413. Adams, Mark S. and Barry Steiner. Energy and the North American Community: Canada, Mexico, and the United States. 3 Hastings Int'l & Comp L. Rev. 369 (1980).

1414. Bledel, E. Food Regulation in Latin America. 28 Food, Drug & C. L. 585 (1973).

1415. Cabrero-Acevedo, Lucio. Legal Protection of the Environment in Mexico. 8 Calif. Wes. Int'l L. J., No. 1 (1978).

1416. Carrillo Prieto, Ignacio and Raúl Nocedal. Legal Protection of the Environment in Developing Countries. Colloquium of the International Association of Legal Science (Mexico, Aug. 25-28, 1974). México: Instituto de Investigationes Jurídicas, UNAM (1976).

1417. "Chile: Blood on the Peaceful Road." 1 Latin American Perspectives no. 2 (Summer 1974).

1418. Comment. Nationalism as a Factor in Legislation Restricting Foreign Investment: Extractive Industries in Mexico. 45 Ind. L. J. 616 (1970).

1419. Commerce Clearing House. Mexican Anti-Pollution Laws and Regulations. New York: Commerce Clearing House (1972).

1420. Daines, David R. and Gonzalo Falconi H. Water Legislation in the Andean Pact Countries. Logan, Utah (1974).

1421. Hydro-electric Resources in Latin America: Their Measurement and Utilization. 7 Econ. Bull. Lat. Am. 73 (1962).

1422. Isbell, Billie Jean. To Defend Ourselves: Ecology and Ritual in an Andean Village. Austin: Univ. of Texas Press (1978).

1423. Johnston, C.C. Effluent Neighbors: The Mexico-United States Water Quality Dilemma. 3 Calif. West. L. Rev. 152 (1952).

1424. Joyner, Christopher C. Latin America's Communal Response to the Energy Crisis: The Latin American Energy Organization (OLADE). 6 Laywer of the Americas 637 (1973).

1425. ___________. US-Mexico Energy Relations in the 1980's. 12 Case Western Res. J. Int'l L. 485 (1980).

1426. Juergensmeyer, J. and E. Blizzard. Legal Aspects of Environmental Control in Mexico. 12 Natural Res. J. 580 (1972).

1427. Ladman, Jerry R., et al., eds. U.S. Mexican Energy Relationships. Lexington: Lexington Books (1981).

1428. Landau, Georges D. The Treaty for Amazonian Cooperation: A Bold New Instrument for Development. 10 Ga. J. Int'l. & Comp. L. 463 (1980).

1429. Levins. Cuba's Emerging Ecology Movement. 1 Cuba Times 12 (Winter 1981).

1430. Lyon, Michael. Modifications in the Water Law of Chile, Contained in the New Agrarian Reform Law. 4 L. & W. L. Rev. 431 (1969).

1431. Martz, John D. and David J. Myers. Venezuela: The Democratic Experience. New York: Praeger (1977).

1432. Mining and Petroleum Legislation of Latin America and the Caribbean. 3rd Ed. General Secretariat, OAS. Dobbs Ferry, NY: Oceana (1979).

1433. Netto, J. M. The Right of Peoples to Dispose of Their Resources: The Situation in Brazil. 8 Rev. Contemp. L. 73 (1961).

1434. Perlman, Janice E. The Myth of Marginality: Urban Politics and Poverty in Rio de Janeiro. Berkeley: Univ. of Calif. Press (1976).

1435. Purpole, Patrick. Firing the Forest. 130 New L. J. 640 (July 17, 1980).

1436. Redick. The Tlateloco Regime and Nonproliferation in Latin America. 35 Int'l Organizations 103 (1981).

1437. Rose, Stanley F. The Development of Peruvian Law for Petroleum Subcontractors. 9 Vanderbilt J. Trans. 579 (1976).

1438. Rossi-Guerrero, Fẹlix P. The Transition from Private to Public Control in the Venezuelan Petroleum Industry. 9 Vanderbilt J. Trans. L. 475 (1976).

1439. Rowles, James P. Nuclear Power and Non-proliferation: The View from Brazil. 14 Vanderbilt J. Transnat. L. 711 (1981).

1440. Steele, Henry B. Historical Perspectives and New Directions in the Exploration of Latin American Petroleum Resources. 9 Vanderbilt J. Trans. L. 523 (1976).

1441. Symposium: Government and Private Enterprise in Latin American Petroleum Development. 9 Vanderbilt J. Trans. L. 473 (1976).

1442. Tropical Deforestation. Hearings Before the Subcommittee on International Organizations of the Committee on Foreign Affairs, U.S. House of Representatives, 96th Cong., 2d Sess., May 7, June 19, Sept. 18, 1980.


## 2. Claims to Equal Membership in the Human Community

### a. Women and the Family in Latin American Law


1443. Arrom, Silvia M. Women and the Family in Mexico City 1800-1857. Ph.D. thesis, Stanford (1977).

1444. Azicri, Max. The Cuban Family Code: Some Observations on Its Innovations and Continuities. 6 *Rev. Soc. L.* 183 (1980).

1445. ___________. Women's Development through Revolutionary Mobilization: A Study of the Federation of Cuban Women. 2 *Int'l J. Women's Stud.* 27 (1979).

1446. Baade, Hans. The Form of Marriage in Spanish North America. 61 *Cornell L. Rev.* 1 (1975).

1447. Barrios de Chungara, Domitila. *Let Me Speak!* Trans Victoria Ortíz. New York: Monthly Review Press (1978).

1448. Barajas, Santiago. *Derecho del Trabajo.* México: UNAM (1981).

1449. Benjamín, Medea and Mandy MacDonald. Women and the Sexual Revolution. 2 Cuba Times No. 4 (1982), p. 1.

1450. Chaney, Elsa M. *Supermadre: Women in Politics in Latin America.* Austin: Univ. of Texas Press (1979).

1451. "The Changing Family Picture." 4 *Cuba Review* No. 4 (1975).

1452. Claiborne, Amanda. Women in El Salvador. *Resist Newsletter* No. 141, June-July: 1-6.

1453. Comité Central del Partido Comunista, Departamento de Orientación Revolucionaria. *A Discusión: Proyecto de Codigo de Familia.* Habana (1974).

1454. Conner, Richard L. Brazilian Marital Property: The Dwindling Community. 23 *Am. J. Comp. L.* 705 (1975).

1455. "Cuba: La Revolución en Marcha." 2 *Latin American Perspectives*, No. 4 (Supp. 1975).

1456. Duff, Ernest A. The Marital Regime in Latin America. 8 *Inter-Am. L. Rev.* 136 (1966).

1457. Elmendorf, Mary L. *Nine Mayan Women: A Village Faces Change.* New York: John Wiley (1979).

1458. *El Salvador: Background to the Crisis.* Cambridge, MA: Central America Information Office (1982).

1459. Espinel, Vilma. "Central Report" in *Memories, Second Congress, Cuban Women's Federation.* Habana: Editorial Orbe (1975).

1460. _________. La Igualdad Plena de la Mujer. *Bohemia* Aug. 22, 1975, p. 46.

1461. Federation of Cuban Women, "Thesis" in Memories, Second Congress, Cuban Women's Federation. Havana: Editorial Orbe (1975).

1462. Fernandez, Bulte. El Derecho de Familia en cien años de revolución. 1 Rev. Cub. Der., No. 1 (1972), p. 129.

1463. Finlay, Olga. The Rights of Children in Cuba. 13 Colum. Human Rights L. Rev. 221 (1982-82).

1464. Fox, Geoffrey. "Honor, Shame and Women's Liberation in Cuba: Views of Working Class Emigre Men," in Female and Male in Latin America, ed. Ann Pescatello Pittsburgh: Univ. of Pittsburgh Press (1973).

1465. Hahner, June E., ed. Women in Latin American History: Their Lives and Views. Los Angeles: UCLA Latin American Center (1976).

1466. Hinestrosa, Fernando. Panorama of Family Law in Colombia. 8 Inter-Am. L. Rev. 213 (1966).

1467. Iglitzin, Lynn B. & Ruth Ross, eds. Women in the World. A Comparative Study. Santa Barbara: Clio Books (1976).

1468. Knaster, Meri. Women in Latin America: The State Of Research, 1975. 11 Latin Amer. Res. Rev. 3 (No. 1, 1976).

1469. Kozol, Jonathan. Children of the Revolution: A Young Teacher in the Cuban Schools. New York: Delacorte Press (1978).

1470. Lavrin, Asunción, ed. Latin American Women: Historical Perspectives. Westport: Greenwood Press (1978).

1471. Latin American Women: One Myth-Many Realities. NACLA Report on The Americas, Vol. 14, No. 5 (Sept.-Oct. 1980).

1472. Le Riverend, Eduardo. El divorcio. Derechos Cubano y Puertorriqueño. 35 Rev. Jur. Univ. Puerto Rico 535 (1966).

1473. Leiner, Marvin, with Robert Ubell. Children are the Revolution: Day Care in Cuba. New York: Viking Press (1974).

1474. Leitinger, Ilse A. Women's Legal Status -- Women's Roles. Paper, 11th Int'l. Cong., Latin American Studies Assn., Mexico City, Sept. 29-Oct. 1, 1983.

1475. Martin, Megan and Susie Willett, eds. Women in Nicaragua. London: Nicaragua Solidarity Campaign (1980).

1476. Martinez de Duran, Sonia. Child Legislation in Colombia. 13 Colum. Human Rights L. Rev. 101 (1981-82).

1477. Meadow, Arnold, et al. Self-Concept, Negative Family Affect, and Delinquency: A Comparison Across Mexican Social Classes. 19 Criminology 434 (1981).

1478. Medeiros Da Fontseca, Romy. The Law & the Condition of Women in Brazil. 8 Col. Human Rights L. Rev. 11 (1976).

1479. Monroy-Cabra, Marco G. Matrimonio Civil y Divorcio en la Legislacion Colombiana. 2d ed. Bogota: Temis (1979).

1480. Muñoz, Carmen Rodriguez de and Elsa Roca de Salonen. Law and the Status of Women in Peru. 8 Colum. Human Rights L.Rev. 207 (1976).

1481. Muñoz, Carmen Rodriguez de and Elsa Roca de Salonen. Law and the Status of Women in Peru. 8 Colum. Human Rights L. Rev. 207 (1976).

1482. Murray, Nicola. Socialism and Feminism: Women and the Cuban Revolution. Feminist Review, No. 2 (1979).

1483. Nutini, Hugo G., et al, eds. Essays on Mexican Kinship. Pittsburgh: Univ. of Pittsburgh Press (1976).

1484. Peral Collado. El proyecto del Codigo de Familia. 3 Rev. Cub. der., No. 8 (1974) p. 31.

1485. Perez, Lisandro. Codigo de Familia, La Mujer en Cuba Socialista. Habana (1977).

1486. Pescatello, Ann, ed. Female and Male in Latin America: Essays. Pittsburgh: Univ. of Pittsburgh Press (1973).

1487. Ramos, Ana. La Mujer y la revoluccion en Cuba. 11 Casa de las Americas, Nos. 65-66 (March-June 1971).

1488. Randall, Margaret. Cuban Women Now: Interviews with Cuban Women. Toronto: Women's Press (1974).

1489. __________. La Mujer cubana en 1974. 15 Casa de las Americas, No. 89 (March-April 1975).

1490. ______________. *Women in Cuba: Twenty Years Later*. Brooklyn: Smyrna Press (1981).

1491. Sanchez-Cordero, A. Cohabitation Without Marriage in Mexico. 29 *Am. J. Comp. L.* 279 (1981).

1492. Sanchez-Figarola. El regimen juridico de proteccion de la maternidad de la trabajadora. 3 *Rev. Cub. Der.*, No. 8 (1974), p. 209.

1493. Status of Women: The United Nations and Mexico. 8 *Calif. Western Int'l L. J.* 93 (1978).

1494. Steffens, Heidi. Notes from Abroad: Cuba The Day Women Took Over Havana. 3 *Ms*. 28 (April 1975).

1495. Stone, Elizabeth, ed. *Women and the Cuban Revolution: Speeches & Documents by Fidel Castro, with Vilma Espinel and Others*. New York: Pathfinder Press (1981).

1496. Suarez Moreno, Jose. El Codigo de Familia. 16 *Verde olivo*, No. 24 (June 16, 1974).

1497. Wald, Karen. *Children of Che: Childcare and Education in Cuba*. Palo Alto: Ramparts Press (1978).

1498. Wells, Carol. Women's Participation in the Central American Revolutions. 10 *Latin American Perspectives* (Winter, 1983), p. 103.

1499. *Women in Latin America: An Anthology from Latin American Perspectives*. Riverside: Latin American Perspectives (1979).

b. *Attitudes towards Indians, Blacks and Other Minorities*

1500. Arens, Richard, ed. *Genocide in Paraguay*. Philadelphia: Temple Univ. Press (1976).

1501. Bartra, Roger. El problema indigena y la ideologia indigenista. 36 *Revista Mexicana de Sociologia* 459 (1974).

1502. Bourgois, Phillipe. Class, Ethnicity and the State Among the Miskitu Amerindians of Northeastern Nicaragua. 8 *Latin American Perspectives*, No. 2 (1981) p. 22.

1503. Bowser, Frederick P. The African Slave in Colonial Peru, 1524-1650. Stanford: Stanford Univ. Press (1974).

1504. Burstein, John N. Ethnic Minorities and the Sandinist Government. 36 J. Int'l Aff. 155 (1982).

1505. Carrillo Flores, Antonio. Mexico and the Indian. 16 Americas 9 (Feb. 1964).

1506. Cardoso, Fernando Henrique. Capitalismo e escravidao no Brasil Meridional: O negro na sociedade escravocrata do Rio Grande do Sul. Sao Paulo: Difusaø Europeia do Livro (1962).

1507. Casas, Bartolomé de las. "The Horrors of the Conquest," in Bartolomé de las Casas: A Selection of His Writings. Trans. and ed. George Sanderlin. New York: Knopf (1971).

1508. Chance, John K. Race and Class in Colonial Mexico. Stanford: Stanford Univ. Press (1978).

1509. Clytus, John, with Jane Ricker. Black Man in Red Cuba. Coral Gables: Univ. of Miami Press (1970).

1510. Coy, P. E. B. Justice for the Indian in Eighteenth Century Mexico. 12 Am. J. Legal Hist. 41 (1968).

1511. Davis, Shelton H. Victims of the Miracle: Development and the Indians of Brazil. Cambridge: Cambridge Univ. Press (1977).

1512. Degler, Carl N. Neither Black Nor White: Slavery and Race Relations in Brazil and the United States. New York: MacMillan (1971).

1513. Domínguez, Jorge I. Racial and Ethnic Relations in the Cuban Armed Forces: A Non-Topic. 2 Armed Forces and Society 273 (Winter 1976).

1514. El Salvador: Background to the Crisis. Ed. Frank Afflitto, et al. Cambridge, MA: Central America Information Office (1982).

1515. Fernandes, Florestan. The Negro in Brazilian Society. Trans. Jacqueline D. Skiles, et al., ed. Phylis A. Eveleth. New York: Columbia Univ. Press (1969).

1516. Foladori, Guillermo. El problema indígena en México. Cuadernos Americanos 27 (Nov.-Dec. 1978).

1517. Gross, David R. The Indian and the Brazilian Frontiers. 36 J. Int'l Aff. 1 (1982).

1518. Harris, Marvin. Patterns of Race in the Americas. New York: Walker (1964).

1519. Heath, Shirley B. Telling Tongues: Language Policy In Mexico. New York: Teachers College Press (1972).

1520. Ianni, Octavio. As metamorfoses do escavo: apogeu e crise da escavatura no Brasil meridional. Sao Paulo: Difusao Europeia de Livro (1962).

1521. Irie, Toraji. History of Japanese Migration to Peru, Part I, trans. and ed., William Himel. 31 Hispanic American Hist Rev. 437 (1951), Vol. 31 (1951) 648 (Part II); Vol. 32 (1952) 73 (Part III).

1522. James, C. L. R. The Black Jacobins: Toussaint L'Ouverture and the San Domingo Revolution. 2d. ed. rev. New York: Vintage Books (1963).

1523. Kelman, Shelly. The Yanomamis: Their Battle for Survival. 36 J. Int'l Aff. 15 (1982).

1524. Knight, Franklin W. Slave Society in Cuba During the Nineteenth Century. Madison: Univ. of Wisconsin Press (1970).

1525. Kubler, George. The Indian Caste of Peru 1795-1940. Washington: Smithsonian (1952).

1526. Land and the Forest Dwelling South American Indian: The Role of National Law. 27 Buffalo L. Rev. 759 (1978).

1527. Margadant, G. Floris. Official Mexican Attitudes Toward the Indians: An Historical Essay. 54 Tul. L. Rev. 964 (1980).

1528. Martz, John D. and David J. Myers, eds. Venezuela: The Democratic Experience. New York: Praeger (1977).

1529. Minorities in the Americas. 9 Latin American Perspective, No. 2 (Spring 1982).

1530. Morner, Magnus. Race Mixture in the History of Latin America. Boston: Little Brown (1967).

1531. Morris, H. Life of Bolivian Indians Remains Hard: Inca Descendants Scratch Out Meager Existence in Plateau. Los Angeles Times, March 31, 1977, Part 1-A, p. 14.

1532. Note, Legal Restrictions on Afro-Indian Relations in Colonial Mexico. 55 J. Negro Hist. 131 (1970).

1533. O'Shaugnessy, Hugh. What Future for the Amerindians of South America? Minority Rights Group Report No. 15. London: Minority Rights Group (1973).

1534. Parry, J. H. and Philip M. Sherlock. A Short History of the West Indies. 3d ed. New York: St. Martin's Press (1971).

1535. Perlman, Janice E. The Myth of Marginality: Urban Poverty and Politics in Rio de Janeiro. Berkeley: Univ. of Cal. Press (1976).

1536. Powell, Thomas G.E. Mexican Intellectuals and the Indian Question, 1876-1911. 48 HAHR 19 (1968).

1537. Reed, Nelson. The Caste War of Yucatan. Stanford: Stanford U. Press (1964).

1538. "Revolutionary Nicaragua." 8 Latin American Perspectives, No. 2 (Spring 1981).

1539. Rout, Leslie B., Jr. Race and Slavery in Brazil. 1 Wilson Quarterly 73 (Autumn 1976).

1540. Salomon, Frank. The Andean Contrast. 36 J. Int'l Aff. 55 (1982).

1541. Stabb, Martin S. Indigenism and Racism in Mexican Thought: 1 J. Inter-Am. Stud. And World Affairs. 405 (1959).

1542. Stein, Stanley J. Vassouras: A Brazilian Coffee County 1850-1890 The Roles of Planter and Slave in a Changing Plantation Society. New York: Atheneum (1970).

1543. Stewart, Watt. Chinese Bondage in Peru: A History of the Chinese Coolie in Peru, 1849-1874. Durham, NC: Duke Univ. Press (1951).

1544. Swepston, Lee. The Indian in Latin America: Approaches to Administration, Integration and Protection. 27 Buffalo L. Rev. 715 (1978).

1545. __________. Latin American Approaches to the "Indian Problem." 117 Int'l Labor Rev. 179 (1978).

1546. Symposium on Inter-Ethnic Conflict in South America, Bridgetown, Barbados, 1971. Geneva: World Council of Churches (Publications of the Dept. of Ethnology, Univ. of Berne, No. 3) (1972).

1547. Toplin, Robert Brent. The Abolition of Slavery in Brazil. New York: Atheneum (1975).

1548. Wagley, Charles and others. Race and Class in Rural Brazil. Paris: UNESCO (1952).

1549. The Yanomami Indian Park. Boston: Anthropology Resource Center (1981).

## 3. Access to the Political Process

### a. Rules Governing the Formation and Behavior of Political Parties and Other Modes of Political Participation

1550. Baloyra, Enrique. El Salvador in Transition. Chapel Hill: Univ. of No. Car. Press (1982).

1551. Berry, R. Albert, Ronald G. Hellman and Mauricio Solaun, eds. Politics of Compromise: Coalition Government in Columbia. New Brunswick: Transaction Books (1980).

1552. Collier, Ruth Berins and David Collier. Inducements versus Constraints: Disaggregating Corporatism. 73 Am. Pol. Sci. Rev. 967 (December, 1979).

1553. Collier, Ruth Berins. Popular Sector Incorporation and Regime Evolution in Brazil and Mexico. Paper presented at the Conference on Brazil and Mexico, Center for Inter-American Relations, New York (1978).

1554. Comité Central del Partido Comunista de Cuba. Departamento de Orientación Revolucionaria. Sobre los órganos del poder popular. Habana: Imprenta Federico Engels (1976).

1555. Cuba: La Revolución en Marcha. 2 Latin American Perspectives, No. 4 (Supp., 1975).

1556. Domínguez, Jorge I. Cuba: Order and Revolution. Cambridge: Harvard Univ. Press (1978).

1557. Dominguez, Jorge I., and Christopher N. Mitchell. The Roads Not Taken: Institutionalization and Political Parties in Cuba and Bolivia. 9 Comparative Politics, 173 (January 1977).

1558. Evans, Peter. Dependent Development: The Alliance of Multinational, State and Local Capital in Brazil. Princeton: Princeton Univ. Press (1979).

1559. Franqui, Carlos. Family Portrait with Fidel: A Memoir. Trans. Alfred MacAdam. New York: Random House (1984).

1560. Gil, Federico Guillermo, et al. Chile at the Turning Point: Lessons of the Socialist Years. Trans. J. Gitlitz. Phila.: ISHI (1979).

1561. Gonzalez Casanova, Pablo. Democracy in Mexico. trans. Danielle Salti. London: Oxford Univ. Press (1970).

1562. Gonzalez, Edward. The Party Congress and Poder Popular: Orthodoxy, Democratization, and the Leader's Dominance. 6 Cuban Studies/Estudios Cubanos (July 1976) p. 1.

1563. __________. Cuba under Castro: The Limits of Charisma. Boston: Houghton Mifflin (1974).

1564. Harnecker, Marta, ed. Cuba: Dictatorship or Democracy? Trans Patrick Greenville. 5th Ed. Westport: Lawrence Hill & Co. (1979).

1565. Herman, Edward S. and Frank Brodhead. Demonstration Elections: US-Staged Elections in the Dominican Republic, Vietnam, and El Salvador. Boston: South End Press (1984).

1566. Huizer, Gerrit. Community Development, Land Reform & Political Participation: Preliminary Observations on Some Cases in Latin America. 28 Am. J. of Eco. & Soc. 159 (1969).

1567. La constitucion de los organos de poder popular. Habana: Imprenta Federico Engels (1974).

1568. Lamounier, Bolivar et al., eds. Direito, Cidadania E. Participacao. Sao Paulo: T.A. Queiroz (1981).

1569. Leogrande, W. L. Party Development in Revolutionary Cuba. 21 J. Int'l Stud. & World Affairs 457 (1979).

1570. Malloy, James M., ed. Authoritarianism and Corporatism in Latin America. Pittsburgh: Univ. of Pittsburgh Press (1977).

1571. Martz, John and David Myers, eds. Venezuela: The Democratic Experience. New York: Praeger (1977).

1572. Mexico in the Eighties. 9 Latin American Perspectives, No. 1 (1982).

1573. McDonald, Ronald H. *Party Systems and Elections in Latin America*. Chicago: Markham Publishing Co. (1971).

1574. O'Donnell, Guillermo A. *Modernization and Bureaucratic-Authoritarianism: Studies in South American Politics*. Berkeley: Institute of Int'l Studies, Univ. of California. (1979).

1575. Powell, Sandra. Political Participation in the Barriadas: A Case Study. 2 *Comp. Pol. Stud.* 195 (1969).

1576. Potash, Robert A. *The Army and Politics in Argentina 1945-1962: Perón to Frondizi*. Stanford: Stanford Univ. Press (1980).

1577. Pratt, Raymond. Parties, Neighborhood Associations, and the Politicization of the Urban Poor in Latin America. 15 *Midwest L. Pol. Sci.* 495 (1971).

1578. Reyna, José Luis, and Richard S. Weinert, eds. *Authoritarianism in Mexico*. Philadelphia: ISHI (1977).

1579. Ruiz Massieu, José F. *Normación constitucional de los partidos políticos en América Latina*. México: UNAM (1974).

1580. Seligson, Mitchell A. and John A. Booth, eds. *Political Participation in Latin America*. 2 Vols. New York: Holmes & Meier (1978-1979).

1581. Stepan, Alfred C., ed. *Authoritarian Brazil*. New Haven: Yale Univ. Press (1973).

1582. ______________. *The State and Society: Peru in Comparative Perspective*. Princeton: Princeton Univ. Press. (1978).

1583. ______________. *The Military in Politics: Changing Patterns in Brazil*. Princeton: Princeton Univ. Press (1971).

1584. Valenzuela, Arturo and J. Samuel Valenzuela, eds. *Chile: Politics and Society*. New Brunswick: Transaction Books (1976).

1585. Wiarda, Howard J. ed. *Politics and Social Change in Latin America: The Distinct Tradition*. 2d ed. rev. Amherst: Univ. of Mass Press (1982).

b. The Conduct of Elections

1586. Armstrong, Robert. El Salvador - Beyond Elections. 16 NACLA Report on the Americas, No. 2 (March-April 1982), p. 2.

1587. Bowdler, George A., with Patrick Cotter. Voter Participation in Central America 1954-1981: An Exploration. Washington: Univ. Press of America (1982).

1588. Cantón, Darío. Elecciones y partidos políticos en la Argentina: historia, interpretación y balance, 1910-1966. Buenos Aires: Siglo Veintiuno Argentina Editores (1973).

1589. Needler, Martin C. The Closeness of Elections in Latin America. 12 Latin American Research Review, No. 1 (1977), p. 115.

1590. Wiarda, Howard J. Critical Elections and Critical Coups: State, Society and the Military in the Processes of Latin American Development. Athens, Ohio: Ohio U., Ctr. for Int'l. Studies (1978).

c. The Right to Criticize: Protection and Persecution of Political Dissent

1591. Alvarez Quiñones. Bourgeois Freedom of the Press? A Joke in Bad Taste. Granma Weekly Rev., Sept. 19, 1976, p. 10.

1592. Bishop, Maurice. A Progressive Lawyer in Power: Free Press and the Role of the Media. 37 Guild Prac. 92 (1980)

1593. Central America Information Office. El Salvador 1982: Elections Without Choice. Paper, Cambridge, MA: Camino (March 1982).

1594. Comblin, Joseph. Doctrina de la Seguridad Nacional. Santiago: Vicaría de la Solidaridad (1979).

1595. Dassin, Joan R. The Brazilian Press and the Politics of Abertura. Paper, 11th Int'l. Congress, Latin American Studies Ass'n. Mexico City, Sept. 20-Oct. 1, 1983.

1596. Drinan, Robert F. Religious and Political Suppression in Argentina. Commonweal (Feb. 18, 1977), p. 103.

1597. Frühling-Ehrlich, Hugo. Repressive Policies and Legal Dissent in Authoritarian Regimes: Chile 1973-1981. Paper, 12th Int'l Pol. Sci. Ass'n Meeting, Rio de Janeiro, August 9-14, 1982.

1598. Galardy. The Myth of bourgeois individual freedoms. Granma Weekly Rev., Sept. 26, 1976, p. 8.

1599. Kovadloff, Jacob. Press Suppression in Argentina: The Timerman Case. 108 USA Today 30 (Sept. 1979).

1600. Lappé, Frances Moore and Joseph Collins. Now We Ca Speak. A Journey through the New Nicaragua. San Francisco: Institute for Food and Development Policy (1982).

1601. Lernoux, Penny. Cry of the People. Garden City: Doubleday (1980).

1602. Montealegre Klenner, Hernan. La Seguridad del Esta los Derechos Humanos. Santiago: Edicion Academia de Humanismo Cristiano (1979).

1603. Organization of American States, Inter-American Commission on Human Rights. Second Report on the Situation of Political Prisoners and Their Relatives in Cuba, OEA/Ser. L/V/11.23, Doc. 6, rev. 1. Washington, D.C.: General Secretariat, OAS, 1970.

1604. Pacheco Gomez, Maximo. Longuen. Santiago: Editorial Aconcagua (1980).

1605. Pages, Jose A. Portrait of a Political Prisoner. 2 Cuba Times No. 1 (1981), p. 9.

1606. Pellet Lastra, Arturo. La Libertad de expresion en el Derecho Argentino y Comparado. Buenos Aires: Abeledo-Perrot (1973).

1607. Pierce, Robert N. Keeping The Flame: Media and Government in Latin America. New York: Hastings House (1979).

1608. Ramirez Mercado, Sergio and Pedro J. Chamorro Barrios. Freedom of the Press in Nicaragua. 12 Caribbean Rev. 20 (Winter 1983).

1609. Samper, Daniel et al. Por Quien Votar? Bogotá: Editorial La Oveja Negra (1982)

1610. Sanchez Bardon. Only Attacks on the Revolution Are Censored. Granma Weekly Rev., Oct. 29, 1978, p.5.

1611. Spence, Jack. Media Coverage of El Salvador's Elections. 13 Socialist Rev. (Mar.-April 1983), p.29.

1612. Stevens, Evelyn P. Protest and Response in Mexico. Cambridge: MIT Press (1974).

1613. Timerman, Jacobo. Prisoner Without a Name, Cell Without a Number. Trans. Tony Talbot. New York: Knopf (distributed by Random House) (1981).

## C. Legal Aspects of Latin American Attitudes Towards The International Community

### 1. General: Latin American Nationalism and the Principles and Protocols of International Law and Politics

1614. Aguilar, Alonso, et al. Politica Mexicana Sobre Inversiones Extranjeras. Mexico: UNAM (1980).

1615. Arevalo, Juan Jose. The Shark and the Sardines. Trans. June Cobb and Raul Osegueda. New York: L. Stuart (1961).

1616. American State Papers: Documents, Legislative and Executive, of the Congress of the United States. 2d Series, Vol. 5. Foreign Relations. Washington, 1858, 245-50 (Monroe Doctrine).

1617. Atkins, G. Pope. Latin America in the International Political System. New York: Free Press (1977).

1618. Alvarez Tabio, Fernando. Politica y Derecho Internacional. La Habana: Editorial Ciencias Sociales (1978).

1619. Baklanoff, Eric N. "International Economic Relations," in Revolutionary Change in Cuba, ed. Carmela Mesa Lago. Pittsburgh: Univ. of Pittsburgh Press (1971).

1620. Banco Nacional de Cuba v. Sabbatino. 376 U.S. 298 (1964).

1621. Barnet, Richard J. Intervention and Revolution: The United States in the Third World. New York: World Publishing Co. (1972).

1622. Bazant, Jan. La industria nacional y el comercio exterior 1842-1851. Mexico: Banco Nacional de Comercio Exterior (1962).

1623. Bialer, Seweryn and Alfred Stepan. Cuba, the U.S. and the Central American Mess. New York Review of Books, May 27, 1982, p. 17.

1624. Blackburn, Robin. "Cuba and the Super Powers," in Patterns of Foreign Influence in the Caribbean, Emmanuel Jehuda de Kadt, ed. London: Oxford Univ. Press (1972).

1625. Blasier, Stewart Cole and Carmelo Mesa-Lago, eds. Cuba in the World. Pittsburgh: Univ. of Pittsburgh Press (1979).

1626. Blasier, Stewart Cole. The Hovering Giant: U.S. Responses to Revolutionary Change in Latin America. Pittsburgh: Univ. of Pittsburgh Press (1976).

1627. Block, Mark A. De Sanchez v. Banco Central de Nicarugua: An Extension of the Restrictive Theory of Sovereign Immunity. 7 N.C. J. Int'l L. A. Com. Reg. 419 (1982).

1628. Bonsal, Philip W. Cuba, Castro, and the United States. Pittsburgh: Univ. of Pittsburgh Press (1971).

1629. Brooke, Jim. Dateline Brazil: Southern Superpower Foreign Policy, Fall 1981, p. 167.

1630. Bulletin, U.S. Dept. of State, April 3, 1961, 471-74 (Alliance for Progress).

1631. Camp, Hope H., Jr. Mexico: Economic Independence as Basis for Ties to the United States. 12 Case W. Res. J. Int'l. L. 453 (1980).

1632. Cardoso, Fernando H. and Enzo Faletto. Dependency and Development in Latin America. Trans. Marjory M. Urquidi. Berkeley: Univ. of Cal. Press (1979).

1633. Castro, Fidel. "La Enmienda Platt: La Constitución de un país sometido," in Juan Rosales, ed., Legalidad y poder Popular en Cuba. Buenos Aires: Editorial Convergencia (1976).

1634. Chaplin, David, ed. Peruvian Nationalism: A Corporatist Revolution. New Brunswick: Transaction Books (1976).

1635. Chavarría, J. Intellectuals and the Crisis of Modern Peruvian Nationalism: 1870-1919. 50 HAHR 257 (1970).

1636. "Chile: Blood On the Peaceful Road," 1 Latin American Perspectives, No. 2 (Summer 1974).

1637. Davis, Harold E., John J. Finan, F. Taylor Peck. Latin American Diplomatic History: An Introduction. Baton Rouge: Louisiana State Univ. Press (1977).

1638. Dawson, Frank G. Contributions of Lesser Developed Nations to International Law: The Latin American Experience. 13 Case W. Res. J. Int'l L. 37 (1981).

1639. De Sanchez v. Banco Nacional de Nicaragua. 515 F. Supp. 900 (E.D. La. 1981).

1640. Dias da Silva, Augustino F. Immunity of Foreign States in Brazilian Labor Courts. 3 Lawyer of the Americas 269 (1971).

1641. Diskin, Martin, ed. Trouble in Our Backyard: Central America and the United States in the Eighties. New York: Pantheon Press (1983).

1642. Dominguez, Jorge I. The United States and Its Regional Security Interests: The Caribbean, Central, and South America. 109 Daedalus 115 (Fall 1980).

1643. ________. Cuban Foreign Policy. 57 Foreign Affairs 83 (1978).

1644. ________, ed. Cuba: Internal and International Affairs. Beverly Hills: Sage (1982).

1645. Drago, Luis. State Loans in Their Relation to International Policy. 1 Am. J. Int'l. L. 605 (1907).

1646. Epstein, Edward C. Introduction to Recent Developments in Mexican Law: Politics of Modern Nationalism. 4 Denver J. Int'l L. & Pol. 1 (1974).

1647. Ex Parte Republic of Peru. 318 U.S. 578 (1943).

1648. Fagg, John Edwin. Pan Americanism. Melbourne, Fla.: Krieger Publishing Co. (1982).

1649. Fagen, Richard R. The Realities of U.S. - Mexican Relations. 55 Foreign Affairs 685 (1977).

1650. The Federal Reserve Act of 1913: Fulcrum For United States Economic Expansion in Latin America. 21 Wayne L. Rev. 1373 (1975).

1651. Ferris, Elizabeth G. and Jennie K. Lincoln, Eds. Latin American Foreign Policies. Boulder: Westview (1979).

1652. Fishlow, Albert. The United States and Brazil: The Case of the Missing Relationship. 60 Foreign Affairs 904 (1982).

1653. Foner, Philip S. A History of Cuba and its Relations with the United States. New York: International Publishers (1962).

1654. Frei Montalvo, Eduardo. The Second Latin American Revolution. 50 Foreign Affairs 83 (1971).

1655. Furtado, Celso. Economic Development of Latin America. Trans. Suzette Macedo. 2d ed. Cambridge: Cambridge Univ. Press (1976).

1656. Gardner, James A. Legal Imperialism: American Lawyers and Foreign Aid in Latin America. Madison: Univ. of Wisconsin Press (1980).

1657. Gellman, Irwin F. Roosevelt and Batista. Good Neighbor Diplomacy in Cuba 1933-1946. Albuquerque: Univ. of New Mexico Press (1973).

1658. Gormley, W. Paul. The Influence of the United States and the OAS on the International Law of Reservations. 7 Inter-Am. L. Rev. 127 (1965).

1659. Governance in the Western Hemisphere. Report, June, 1982, Aspen Institute for Humanistic Studies, New York, N.Y.

1660. Graham, Richard. Britain and the Onset of Modernization in Brazil, 1850-1914 Cambridge: Cambridge Univ. Press (1968).

1661. Grunwald, Joseph, ed. Latin America in the International System. Beverly Hills: Sage Publications (1980).

1662. Gutiérrez-Gutiérrez, Carlos José. Conflicts between Domestic and International Law. 30 American U. L. Rev. 147 (1980).

1663. Hamlin, Wilbur G., Jr. Panama Canal - Legal Issues Involved in the Transfer of the Canal to Panama. 19 Harvard Int'l L. J. 279 (1978).

1664. Horowitz, Irving Louis, ed. Cuban Communism. 4th ed. New Brunswick: Transaction Books (1981).

1665. Jacobini, H.B. International Law in Latin America. 7 Lawyer of the Americas 605 (1975).

1666. ___________. A Study of the Philosophy of International Law as Seen in the Works of Latin American Writers. The Hague: Nijhoff (1954).

1667. Jova, Joseph J. Private Investment in Latin America: Renegotiating the Bargain. 10 Texas Int'l. L. J. 455 (1975).

1668. Langguth, A.J. Hidden Terrors: The Truth about U.S. Police Operations in Latin America. New York: Pantheon (1978).

1669. Lateef, Noel. Parliamentary Diplomacy and the North-South Dialogue. 11 Ga. J. Int'l & Comp. L. 1 (1981).

1670. Latin American Law Symposium: United States and Latin America - Continuity and Change in the Relationship. 12 Calif. West. Int'l L. J. 397 (1982).

1671. LeoGrande, William M. Cuba Policy Recycled. Foreign Policy 46 (Spring 1982).

1672. Letelier v. Republic of Chile. 488 F. Supp. 665 (D.D.C. 1980), 502 F. Supp. 259 (D.D.C. 1980).

1673. Levesque, Jacques. L'URSS et la Revolution Cubaine. Paris: Presses de La Fondation Nationale des Sciences Politiques (1976).

1674. Levin, Jonathan V. The Export Economies: Their Pattern of Development in Historical Perspective. Cambridge: Harvard Univ. Press (1960).

1675. Lowenthal, Abraham F. and Albert Fishlow. Latin America's Emergence: Toward a U.S. Response. (New York: Foreign Policy Association, Headline Series 243, 1979).

1676. Lowenthal, Abraham F. The Caribbean. 6 Wilson Quarterly (Spring 1982) p. 112.

1677. ______________. "U.S.-Latin American Relations in the 1980s." The National Interests of The United States in Foreign Policy, ed. Prosser Gifford. Washington, DC: Woodrow Wilson International Center for Scholars (1981), p. 73.

1678. ______________, ed. The Peruvian Experiment: Continuity and Change Under Military Rule. Princeton: Princeton Univ. Press (1975).

1679. Lozoya, Jorge and Jaime Estévez, eds. Latin America and the New International Economic Order. New York: Pergamon (1980).

1680. Manchester, Alan K. British Preeminence in Brazil, Its Rise and Decline: A Study in European Expansion. Chapel Hill: Univ. of North Carolina Press (1933).

1681. Martí, José. Inside the Monster. Ed. Philip Foner. Trans. Elinor Randall. New York: Monthly Review (1977).

1682. _________. Our America. Trans. Elinor Randall, et al. Ed. Philip Foner. New York: Monthly Review. (1977)

1683. Martz, John D. and David J. Myers, Eds, Venezuela: The Democratic Experience. New York: Praeger (1977).

1684. Mathew, W.M. Peru and the British Guano Market, 1840-1870. 23 Economic History Rev. 112 (1970).

1685. Menges, Constantine C. "The United States and Latin America in the 1980s," in The National Interests of the United States in Foreign Policy, Ed. P. Gifford, Washington: Wilson Int'l Center for Scholars (1981), p. 53.

1686. "Mexico's Macho Mood." Time, Oct. 8, 1979, p. 50.

1687. Moshe, Sanford. Latin American and the World Economy, 1850-1914. Inter-American Economic Affairs, II (1968).

1688. Mower, A. Glenn, Jr. The European Community and Latin America: A Case Study in Global Role Expansi Westport, Ct.: Greenwood Press (1982).

1689. Note, The Letelier Case: Foreign Sovereign Liabili for Acts of Political Assassination. 21 Va. J. Int'l. L. 251 (1981).

1690. Oliver, Covey T. The Gringo's Light Switch and Human, Political and Security Relationships in the New World South and East of the United States. 17 Willamette L. Rev. 185 (1980).

1691. Participation of the USA with the Republics of Latin America in the Common Heritage of Roman and Civil Law. 10 Proc. of 8th American Scientific Congress 467, Washington, D.C.: U.S. Dep't of State (1943).

1692. Pastor, Robert A. Our Real Interests in Central America. The Atlantic (July 1982), p. 27.

1693. Petersen, Gustav H. Latin America: Benign Neglect is Not Enough. 51 Foreign Affairs 598 (1973).

1694. Petras, James. Critical Perspectives on Imperialism and Social Class in the Third World. New York: Monthly eview Press (1978).

1695. Republic of Mexico v. Hoffman. 324 U.S. 30 (1945).

1696. The Rockefeller Report on the Americas. New York Times ed. Chicago: Quadrangle Books (1969).

1697. Rosenn, Keith S. Enforcement of Foreign Arbitral Awards in Brazil. 28 Am. J. Comp. L. 498 (1980).

1698. Rubin, Howard M. The Panama Canal Treaties: Keys to the Locks. 4 Brooklyn J. Int'l L. 159 (1978).

1699. Schlesinger, Stephen and Stephen Kinzer. Bitter Fruit: The Untold Story of the American Coup in Guatemala. Garden City, N.Y.: Doubleday (1982).

1700. Schneyer, Paul A. and Virginia Barta. The Legality of the U.S. Economic Blockade of Cuba under International Law. 13 Case W. Res. J. Int'l L. 451 (1981).

1701. Schoutz, Lars. Human Rights and United States Policy Toward Latin America. Princeton: Princeton Univ. Press (1981).

1702. Silvert, Kalman H. Nationalism in Latin America. 334 American Academy of Political Science 1 (1961).

1703. Smit, Hans. The Proposed Panama Canal Treaties: A Triple Failure. 17 Columbia J. Transnat'l L. 1 (1978).

1704. Smith, Wayne S. Dateline Havana: Myopic Diplomacy. Foreign Policy, No. 48 (Fall 1982), 157.

1705. United States v. United Mexican States. Opinions of Commissioners 21, 1927 (General Claims Commission 1926).

1706. U.S. Senate, Committee on Foreign Relations, 93rd Cong., 1st Sess., March 20-22, 27-29, Apr. 2, 1973, Hearing Before Subcommittee on Multinational Corporations. Multinational Corporations and U.S. Foreign Policy: Parts I and II. 2 vols. Washington, DC: Government Printing Office (1973).

1707. U.S. Senate, Select Committee to Study Governmental Operations with Respect to Intelligence Activities, 94th Congress, 1st Session, Nov. 20, 1975. Alleged Assassination Plots Involving Foreign Leaders. Washington DC: Government Printing Office (1975).

1708. U.S. Senate, 94th Cong. 1st Sess., Dec. 18, 1975. Staff Report of Senate, Select Committee to Study Government Operations. Covert Action in Chile, 1963-1973. Washington, DC: Government Printing Office (1975).

1709. U.S. House of Representatives, 94th Congress, 1st Session, May 8, 13, 15, 20, 22, June 11, 26, July 9, Sept. 23, 1975. Hearings Before the Subcomm. on Int'l Trade and Commerce and Subcomm. on Int'l Organizations. U.S. Trade Embargo of Cuba. Washington, DC: Government Printing Office (1976).

1710. U.S. Dept. of State. Events in the U.S. - Cuban Relations: A Chronology 1957-1963. Washington, D.C.: U.S. Gov't Printing Office (1963).

1711. Weinstein, Martin, ed. Revolutionary Cuba in the World Arena. Philadelphia: ISHI (1979).

1712. Wiarda, Howard J.. Law and Political Development in Latin America: Toward a Framework for Analysis. 19 Am. J. Comp. L. 434 (1971).

1713. Wood, Bryce. The Making of the Good Neighbor Policy. New York: Columbia University Press (1961).

2. Treatment of Aliens

a. The Foreign Investor

1) General

1714. Altmann, M. R. Investing in Brazil. 5 Lawyer of the Americas 499 (1973).

1715. American Bar Association, Sec. on International Law. Current Legal Aspects of Doing Business with Latin America. Chicago: ABA (1981).

1716. Angulo, Manuel R. Comments on the Status of Foreign Business Corporations under the Commercial Codes of Argentina and Venezuela. 4 Inter-Am. L. Rev. 159 (1962).

1717. Araujo Cintra, Antonio Carlos de. Investor's Remedies under the New Brazilian Corporation Act. 9 Lawyer of the Americas 531 (1977).

1718. Armstrong, Robert and Janet Shenk. El Salvador: The Face of Revolution. Boston: South End Press (1982).

1719. Baer, Werner. Import Substitution and Industrialization in Latin America: Experiences and Interpretations. 7 Latin American Res. Rev., no. 1 (Spring, 1972), p. 95.

1720. Barnes, William S. Legal Issues in Inter-American Relations. 11 Texas Int'l L. J. 63 (1976).

1721. Benítez, R. C. United States Investment in Latin America. 5 Lawyer of the Americas 1 (1973).

1722. Bernstein, Marvin, ed. Foreign Investment in Latin America: Cases and Attitudes. New York: Knopf (1966).

1723. Bomchil, Máximo, Jr. New Foreign Investment Regime in Argentina. 7 Brooklyn J. Int'l L. 27 (1981).

1724. Business Perspectives on Latin America. Hearing before the Subcommittee on Inter-American Affairs of the Committee on Foreign Affairs, U.S. House of Representatives, 97th Cong., 1st Sess., April 28, 1981.

1725. Camil, Jorge. The Nationalized Banking System and Foreign Debt [Mexico]. 18 Int'l Lawyer 323 (1984).

1726. Cassinelli, Muñoz N. A Statement of the Laws of Uruguay in Matters Affecting Business. 5th ed. Washington: Pan American Union, General Secretariat, Organization of American States (1971).

1727. Collier, David, ed. The New Authoritarianism in Latin America. Princeton: Princeton Univ. Press (1979).

1728. Dabinovic, Tomislavo E. J.P. Foreign Investments: Politics and International Law. 5 Lawyer of the Americas 10 (1973).

1729. Dahl, Enrique. Argentina's System of Foreign Investments. 6 Fordham Int'l L.J. 33 (1982)

1730. Danino, Roberto. Regulating the Multinational: A Note on the Divestment Myth. 10 Lawyer of the Americas 385 (1978).

1731. Dos Santos, Theotonio. "The Changing Structure of Foreign Investments in Latin America," in James Petras and Maurice Zeitlin, eds., Latin America: Reform or Revolution? Greenwich, Conn.: Fawcett Publications (1968).

1733. Felix, David. Monetarists, Structuralists, and Import-Substituting Industrialization: A Critical Approach. Studies in Comparative International Development, no. 10 (1965).

1734. Fabre, Mary E. Bribery and the Multinationals in Latin America: Only the Tip of the Iceberg. 10 *Laywer of the Americas* 371 (1978).

1734. Felsberg, Thomas B. *Foreign business in Brazil: a practical law guide*. 2nd ed. Sao Paulo: Instituto Brasileiro de Direito Transnacional (1976).

1735. Fernández Arena, José Antonio and Herbert May. *Impact of Foreign Investment In Mexico*. Washington, D.C.: National Chamber Foundation (1971).

1736. Fishlow, Albert. "The Mature Neighbor Policy," in *Latin America and World Economy: A Changing International Order*. ed. Joseph Grunwald. Beverly Hills: Sage Publications (1978).

1737. Fontaine, Roger W. *On Negotiating with Cuba*. Washington: American Enterprise Institute for Public Policy Research (1975).

1738. Franko, Lawrence B. "Joint International Business Ventures in Developing Countries," in *Latin America-U.S. Economic Interactions*, ed. Robert B. Williamson, et al. Washington: American Enterprise Institute for Public Policy Research (1974).

1739. French-Davis, Ricardo. "Foreign Investment in Latin America: Recent Trends and Prospects," in *Latin America in the International Economy*, ed. Vićtor Urquidi and Rosemary Thorp. New York: Wiley (1973).

1740. Frieden, Jeff. Third World Indebted Industrialization: International Finance and State Capitalism in Mexico, Brazil, Algeria, and South Korea. 35 *Int. Organization* 407 (1981).

1741. Girling, Robert H. Nicaragua's Commerical Policy. Building a Socially Responsive Foreign Trade. 10 *Latin American Perspectives* (Winter 1983), p. 33.

1742. Giacchino, Ricardo. Foreign Investment under Contemporary Argentine Law. 26 *Am. J. Comp. L.* 91 (1977).

1743. Gordon, Michael W. Observations on the Nature of Joint Ventures in Mexico: Are They Involuntary and Transitory Institutions? 2 *Boston Coll. Int'l & Comp. L. Rev.* 337 (1979).

1744. ______________. *Latin American Trade and Investment*. 5th ed. Gainesville: Univ. of Florida (1979).

1745. ______________, ed. Materials on International Conflicts in the Western Hemisphere. 3d ed. Gainesville: Univ. of Florida (1981).

1746. Hunt, Shane. "Direct Foreign Investment in Peru," in The Peruvian Experiment: Continuity and Change Under Military Rule, ed. Abraham F. Lowenthal. Princeton: Princeton Univ. Press (1975).

1747. Investment, Lending and Legal Issues of Doing Business in Latin America in the 1980's. New York: Law Journal Seminar Press (1979).

1748. Jova, Joseph J., Clint E. Smith, T. Frank Crigler. Private Investment in Latin America: Renegotiating The Bargain. 19 Tex. Int'l. L.J.3 (1984).

1749. Laughran, Harry S. and Jack V. Foster, Jr. Foreign Investment in Mexico: The Emergency Decrees of 1944. 39 Tulane L. Rev. 538 (1965).

1750. Martz, John and David J. Myers, eds. Venezuela: The Democratic Experience. New York: Praeger (1977).

1751. McKinnis, George C. The Argentine Foreign Investment Law of 1976. 17 Colum. J. Transnat'l L. 357 (1978).

1752. Measures Strengthening the Negotiating Capacity of Governments in their Relations with Transnational Corporations: Joint Ventures Among Firms in Latin America. New York: United Nations Centre on Transnational Corporations (1983).

1753. "Mexico in the Eighties." 9 Latin American Perspectives, no. 1 (Winter, 1982).

1754. Moran, Theodore H. Multinational Corporations and the Politics of Dependence: Copper in Chile. Princeton: Princeton Univ. Press (1974).

1755. The Multinational Corporation in Latin America: Selected Readings. Gainesville, Fl.: Mexican Summer Law Program, University of Florida and Escuela Libra de Derecho, Mexico (1981).

1756. Murphy, Ewell E., Jr. U.S. Trade and Investment in Mexico: An Overview of the Eighties. 12 Lawyer of the Americas 573 (1980).

1757. ______. Drafting Mexican-U.S. Commercial Agreements. 5 Int'l Lawyer 577 (1971).

1758. Nattier, Frank E. Regulation of Transnational Corporations: Latin American Actions in International Fora. 19 Tex. Int'l L.J. 265 (1984).

1759. Odell, John S. Latin American Trade Negotiations with the United States. 34 Int'l Organization 207 (1980).

1760. "Peru: Bourgeois Revolution and Class Struggle." 4 Latin American Perspectives, no. 3 (1977).

1761. Pinheiro Neto, J.M. Multinationals in Brazil. 8 Case West. Res. J. Int'l L. 311 (1976).

1762. Pinheiro Neto, J.M. and Irene Dias da Silva. Incentives for Investment in Brazil. 13 Case West Res. J. Int'l L. 123 (1981).

1763. Pitts, Gary B. American Investment in Mexico. 2 Houston J. Int'l L. 261 (1980).

1764. Price, Waterhouse and Company. Doing Business in Columbia. New York: Price, Waterhouse and Compan (1973).

1765. "Public Debt and Private Profit: International Finance in Peru and Argentina." 12 NACLA Report on the Americas (July-August, 1978).

1766. Radway, Robert J. Doing Business in Mexico: A Practical Legal Analysis. 14 Int'l Lawyer 361 (1980).

1767. Radway, Robert J. and Franklin T. Holt-Linares. Venezuela Revisited: Foreign Investment, Technology, and Related Issues. 15 Vanderbilt J. Transnat'l L. 1 (1982).

1768. Rooney, John H., Jr. The United States-Mexico Trade Agreement of 1977. 13 Texas Int'l L. J. 435 (1978).

1769. Rose, Stanley F. The Peruvian Revolution's Approach: Investment Policy and Climate 1968-1980 Buffalo: W.S. Hein (1981).

1770. Rosenn, Keith S. Regulation of Foreign Investment in Brazil: A Critical Analysis. 15 Lawyer of America. 307 (1983).

1771. Rowland, Walter S. Foreign Investment in Brazil: A Reconciliation of Perspectives. 14 J. Int'l Law and Econ. 39 (1979).

1772. Saddy, Fehmy, ed. Arab Latin American Relations: Energy, Trade and Investment. New Brunswick: Transaction Books (1983).

1773. Shea, Donald R. et al., eds. Reference Manual on Doing Business in Latin America. Milwaukee: Univ. of Wis. Center for Latin America (1979).

1774. Skola, Thomas J. Foreign Loans in Brazil: Theory and Practice. 15 Int'l Lawyer 73 (1981).

1775. Stallings, Barbara. Latin American Debt: What Kind of Crisis? 3 Sais Rev. 27 (No.2) (1983).

1776. Tugwell, Franklin. The Politics of Oil in Venezuela. Stanford: Stanford Univ. Press (1975).

1777. U.S. Department of Commerce. Bureau of East-West Trade. United States Commercial Relations with Cuba: A Survey. Washington, D.C.: U.S. Government Printing Office (1975).

1778. U.S. Department of Commerce. Establishing a Business in Ecuador. Washington, D.C.: U.S. Government Printing Office (1960).

1779. U.S.-Mexico Trade Law Conference. Federal Bar Ass'n., Dallas, March 19-20, 1980.

1780. Vázquez Pando, Fernando. Legal Aspects of Mexican Exchange Controls. 18 Int'l Lawyer 309 (1984).

1781. Wallace, M., ed. Multinational Corporations Law: Mexico, Central America, Panama and the Central American Common Market. Dobbs Ferry: Oceana Pub. (1981).

1782. Wurfel, Seymour. Foreign Enterprise in Colombia: Laws and Policies. Chapel Hill: Univ. of North Carolina Press (1965).

1783. Zorn, Jean G. and Harold Mayerson. The Caribbean Basin Initiative: A Windfall for the Private Sector. 14 Lawyer of the Americas 523 (1983).

2. Nationalization and Expropriation of Property

1784. Baklanoff, Eric N. Expropriation of U.S. Investments in Cuba, Mexico and Chile. New York: Praeger (1975).

1785. Barona Lobato, Juan. La Expropriación Petrolera. Tlatelolco, México: Secretaria de Relaciones Exteriores (1974).

1786. Bermúdez, Antonio J. The Mexican National Petroleum Industry: A Case Study in Nationalization. Stanford: Hispanic American and Luso-Brazilian Studies (1963).

1787. Borchard, Edwin. The "Minimum Standard" of the Treatment of Aliens. 38 Michigan L. Rev. 445 (1940).

1788. Casad, Robert C. and Rogelio Sotela Montagné. Expropriation in Central America and Panama Processes and Procedures. Buffalo: W.S. Hein (1975).

1789. Casad, Robert C. Expropriation Procedures in Central America. 8 Int'l Lawyer 316 (1974).

1790. Connell-Smith, Gordon. The United States and Latin America: An Historial Analysis of Latin-American Relationships. London: Heinemann Educat. Books (1974).

1791. Corporación del Cobre. Negociaciones con las Empresas Americanas del Cobre Afectadas por la Nacionalización de 1971. Santiago (1974).

1792. Díaz-Alezandro, Carlos. "Direct Foreign Investment in Latin America," in The International Corporation: A Symposium. Charles Pour Kindleberger, ed. Cambridge: MIT Press (1970).

1793. Eder, George J. Expropriation: Hickenlooper and Hereafter. 4 Int'l Lawyer 611 (1970).

1794. Einhorn, Jessica. Expropriation Politics. Lexington, MA. Lexington Books (1974).

1795. Freeman, Alwyn V. The International Responsibility of States for Denial of Justice. London: Longmans Green & Co. (1938).

1796. Furnish, Dale B. Eder's Hickenlooper: Some Clarifications Regarding Peru and Other Matters. 5 Int'l Lawyer 348 (1971).

1797. Gantz, David A. The Marcona Settlement: New Forms of Negotiations and Compensation for Nationalized Property. 71 Am. J. Int'l L. 474 (1977).

1798. __________. Dispute Settlement. 73 Proc. Am. Soc'y Int'l L. 249 (1979).

1799. Girvan, Norman. The Question of Compensation: A Third World Perspective. 5 *Vanderbilt J. Transnat'l L.* 340 (1972).

1800. González-Chaparro, Camilo. *Foreign Investment in Columbia: Basic Rules*. Trans. Hanka de Rhodes. Bogotá: Departamento Nacional de Planeación (1979).

1801. Gordon, Michael W. Argentine Jurisprudence: The Parke Davis and Deltec Cases. 6 *Lawyer of the Americas* 320 (1974).

1802. ______. The Settlement of Claims for Expropriated Foreign Private Property Between Cuba and Foreign Nations other than the United States. 5 *Lawyer of the Americas* 457 (1973).

1803. ______. *The Cuban Nationalizations: The Demise of Foreign Private Property*. Buffalo: Wm. S. Hein (1976).

1804. Huerta, John E. Peruvian Nationalization & the Peruvian-American Compensation Agreements. 10 *N.Y.U. J. Int'l L. & Pol.* 1 (1977).

1805. Ingram, George M. *Expropriation of U.S. Property in South America: Nationalization of Oil and Copper Companies in Peru, Bolivia and Chile*. New York: Praeger (1974).

1806. Kennecott Copper Corporation. *Expropriation of El Teniente*. New York (1971).

1807. Kennecott Copper Corporation. *Confiscation of El Teniente*. 4 supplements. New York (1971-1973).

1808. Lillich, Richard B. The Recent Chilean Experience and Future Prospects. 2 *Denver J. Int'l L. and Policy* 136 (1972).

1809. ______. International Law and the Nationalizations - the Valuation of the Copper Companies. 7 *Int'l Lawyer* 124 (1973).

1810. Lowenfeld, Andreas, ed. *Expropriation in the Americas: A Comparative Study*, New York: Dunellen (1971).

1811. Merino Brito. Contratación Económica y Planificación. 2 *Rev. Cub. Jur.* 5 (1963).

1812. Miranda, F. Mexican Tax Incentives for "Mexicanized" Companies. 25 *Tax Lawyer* 419 (1972).

1813. Moran, Theodore H. Multinational Corporations and the Politics of Dependence: Copper in Chile. Princeton: Princeton Univ. Press (1974).

1814. More-Benítez. Nationalization an Instrument of Socialisation in the Cuban Revolution. 8 Rev. Contemp. L. 95 (1961).

1815. Orrego-Vicuña, Francisco. Some International Law Problems Posed by the Nationalization of the Copper Industry by Chile. 67 Am. J. Int'l L. 711 (1973).

1816. Piper, Don C. On Changing or Rejecting the International Legal Order. 12 Int'l Lawyer 293 (1978).

1817. Rabinowitz, Víctor. International Law and Compensation for Expropriation: Cuba. 31 Guild Prac. 90 (1974).

1818. Rosenn, Keith S. Expropriation in Argentina and Brazil: Theory and Practice. 15 Virginia J. Int'l L. 277 (1975).

1819. ________. Expropriation, Inflation and Development. 1972 Wisconsin L. Rev. 845 (1972).

1820. Shea, Donald R. The Calvo Clause: A Problem of International Law and Diplomacy. Minneapolis: Univ. of Minnesota Press (1955).

1821. Sigmund, Paul E. Multinationals in Latin America: The Politics of Nationalization. Madison: Univ. of Wisconsin Press (1980).

1822. Smith, David N. and Louis T. Wells, Jr. Negotiating Third World Mineral Agreements: Promises As Privilege. Cambridge, MA: Ballinger (1975).

1823. Symposium: Expropriation. 2 Denver J. Int'l L. and Policy 125 (1972).

1824. Thome, Joseph R. The Colombian Agrarian Reform: Legal Limitations on the Process of Expropriation. 8 Inter-Am L. Rev. 269 (1966).

1825. Tugwell, Franklin. The Politics of Oil in Venezuela. Stanford: Stanford Univ. Press (1975).

1826. Wortley, Ben A. Expropriation in Public International Law. Cambridge: University Press (1959).

1827. Yates, Harvey. Condemnation in the U.S. and Expropriation in Venezuela: A Comparative Legal Study. 6 Lawyer of the Americas 259 (1974).

3) Restrictions on Foreign Investment


1828. Antezana, Mario H. and Michael D. Butterman. Private Investment in Bolivia: Organizing to do Business. 6 Inter-Am. L. Rev. 265 (1964).

1829. Aracama Zorraqui, E.d. The New Argentine Law on the Transfer Assignment or Licensing of Technology or Trademarks. 17 Ind. Prop'y. 24 (1978).

1830. Bernstein, Marvin D., ed. Foreign Investment in Latin America: Cases and Attitudes. New York: Knopf (1966).

1831. Browning, David S. Historic Basis of Mexican Mining Law. 7 Inter. Am. L. Rev. 1 (1965).

1832. Bulson, Michael E. Mexico's Border Industrial Program: Legal Guidelines for the Foreign Investor. 4 Denver J. Int'l L. & Policy 89 (1974).

1833. Caraza Escobedo, Rafael. Taxation of the Extractive Industries: National Report: Mexico. 63A Cahiers de Droit Fisc. Int'l. 391 (1978).

1834. Cervin, Bennett W. Requirements for Local Participation in Private Direct Foreign Investments in Mexico. 33 Texas B. J. 609 (1970).

1835. Colloquium on Certain Legal Aspects of Foreign Investment in Mexico. 7 Georgia J. Int'l & Comp. L. 1 (1977).

1836. Comment. Nationalism as a Factor in Legislation Restricting Foreign Investment: Extractive Industries in Mexico. 45 Ind. L. J. 616 (1970).

1837. Comment. The United States - Mexico Trade Agreement of 1977. 13 Texas Int'l L. J. 435 (1978).

1838. Doing Business in Brazil. New York: Price Waterhouse and Company (1980).

1839. Doing Business in Columbia. New York: Price, Waterhouse and Company (1978).

1840. Fisher, Stewart. The Regulation of Foreign Business in Mexico: Recent Legislation in Historical Perspective. 7 N.C.J. Int'l La. Com. Reg. 383 (1982).

1841. French, Jan Hoffman. Brazil's Profit Remittance Law: Reconciling Goals in Foreign Investments. 14 L. & Pol. Int'l Bus. 399 (1982).

1842. Gómez-Palacio, Ignacio. Defining "New Lines of Products" Under Mexico's Foreign Investment Law. 8 Calif. Western Int'l L. J. 74 (1978).

1843. González-Chaparro, Camilo. Foreign Investment in Columbia: Basic Rules. Trans. Hanka de Rhodes. Bogotá: Departmento Nacional de Planeación (1979).

1844. Gordon, Michael W. The Contemporary Mexican Approach to Growth with Foreign Investment: Controlled But Participatory Independence. 10 Calif. Western L. Rev. 1 (1973).

1845. __________. The Joint Venture as an Institution for Mexican Development: A Legislative History. 2 Arizona St. L. J. 173 (1978).

1846. Grunwald, Joseph. Foreign Private Investment: The Challenge of Latin American Nationalism. 11 Virginia J. Int'l L. 228 (1971).

1847. Hollman, Stephen N. Mexican Restrictions on Foreign Investment and Technology. 20 Pract. Lawyer 55 (Feb. 1974).

1848. Inman, Harry A. U.S.-Mexican Trade: New initiatives are needed now. 7 N.C. J. Int'l L. & Com. Reg. 335 (1982).

1849. Jova, Joseph J. Private Investment in Latin America: Renegotiating the Bargain. 10 Texas Int'l L. J. 455 (1975).

1850. Juncadella, Salvador. Establishing Branches of Foreign Corporations in Central America, Panama and British Honduras. 1 Lawyer of the Americas 21 (1969).

1851. ___________. Legislation on Antimonopoly and Unfair Competition: Central America and Panama. 8 Lawyer of the Americas 60 (1976).

1852. Juttner, H. Legal Safeguards for Direct Investment in LDC's. 9 Inter. Economics 259 (1976).

1853. Leacock, Stephen. J. Essentials of Investor Protection in the Commonwealth Caribbean and the United States. 6 Lawyer of the Americas 662 (1974).

1854. Morales-Hernández, Alfredo. Foreign Investment and Banking in Latin America. 5 Lawyer of the Americas 16 (1973).

1855. Ness, W. L. Brazil: Local Equity Participation in Multinational Enterprises. 6 Law & Pol. Int'l Bus. 1017 (1974).

1856. Pacheco, Humberto. Foreign Investment in Costa Rica: The Legal Framework. 3 Lawyer of the Americas 246 (1971).

1857. Quale, Andrew C. Jr. U.S. Bank Operations in Latin America: The Legal Environment. Paper, Center for Int'l Banking Studies, Conference on Latin American Update, March 9-10, 1981.

1858. Radway, Robert J. Comparative Evaluation of Technology Transfer in Latin America: The Practical Realities. 9 Denver J. Int'l L. & Pol. 197 (1980).

1859. ______________. Negotiating with Latin American Governments: Technology Transfer and Service Agreements. 76 Pat. & Tm. Rev. 271 (1978).

1860. Ritch, James E. Legal Aspects of Activities of Foreign Financial Institutions in Mexico. 8 Calif. Western Int'l L. J. 60 (1978).

1861. ______________. Legal Aspects of Lending to Mexican Borrowers. 7 N.C.J. Int'l L. Com. Reg. 315 (1982).

1862. Rogers, W. D. Of Missionaries, Fanatics and Lawyers: Some Thoughts on Investment Disputes in the Americas. 72 Am. J. Int'l L. 1 (1978).

1863. Rose, S. F. Business Operations in Peru. Leonard L. Silverstein, Ed. Washington, D.C.: Tax Management (No. 329) (1975).

1864. Rosenn, Keith S. Adjusting Taxation of Business Income for Inflation: Lessons from Brazil and Chile. 13 Texas Int'l L. J. 165 (1978).

1865. Schill, Charles F. The Mexican and Andean Investment Codes: An Overview and Comparison. 6 Law & Policy Int'l Bus. 437 (1974).

1866. Schmitz, John W. Profit Sharing in Mexico. 10 Lawyer of the Americas 99 (1978).

1867. Seixas, Delio de. Brazil's Law on Foreign Capital. 5 Lawyer of the Americas 513 (1973).

1868. Siqueiros, José L. The Juridical Regulation of Transnational Enterprises. 8 Calif. Western Int'l L. J. 1 (1978).

1869. Soberanis, Jaime A. The Changing Legal Climate for Multinational Investments in Developing Countries. 10 Lawyer of the Americas 365 (1978).

1870. Studwell, Thomas W. and Guillermo Cabonellas. The New Argentine Foreign Investment Law: An Analysis and Commentary. 1 Hasting Int'l & Comp. L. Rev. 37 (1977).

1871. Tancer, Robert S. and John P. Zanotti. The Mexican Law of Foreign Real Estate Investment in the Prohibited Zones. An Overview 1971-73. 2d ed., Tempe: Arizona State Univ. Press (1975).

1872. Trade and Credit in Latin America: Problems and Resolutions. 2d ed. New York: Chase Trade Information Corporation (1981).

1873. Trading in Latin America: The Impact of Changing Policies. New York: Business International Corp. (1981).

1874. Trevino, Julio C. Mexico: The Present Status of Legislation and Government Policy on Direct Foreign Investment. 18 Int'l Lawyer 297 (1984).

1875. Vilaplana, Víctor A. The Forbidden Zones in Mexico. 10 Calif. West. L. Rev. 47 (1973).

1876. Wallace, M., ed. Multinational Corporation Law: Mexico, Central America, Panama, and the Central American Common Market, Dobbs Ferry: Oceana (1981).

1877. Wehberg, Hans. Pacta Sunt Servanda. 53 Am. J. Int'l L. 775 (1959).

1878. Wurfel, Seymour W. Foreign Enterprise in Columbia: Laws and Policies. Chapel Hill: Univ. of North Carolina Press (1965).

1879. Xavier, Alberto. The Taxation of Foreign Investment in Brazil. Deventer: Kluwer (1980) (Series on Int'l Taxation No. 1).

1880. Zamora, Stephen. Peso-Dollar Economics and the Imposition of Foreign Exchange Controls in Mexico. 32 Am. J. Comp. L. 99 (1984).

1881. Zorn, Jean G. and Harold A. Mayerson. Cuba's Joint Venture Law: New Rules for Foreign Investment. 21 Colum. J. Transnat'l L. 273 (1983).

4. Restrictions on the Transfer of Technology


1882. Alvarez-Soberanis, Jaime. La Regulación de las Invenciones y Marcas y de la Transferencia de Tecnología. México: Ed. Porrúa (1979).

1883. Blair, Homer O. Technology Transfer as an Issue in North-South Negotiations. 14 Vand. J. Transnat'l L. 301 (1981).

1884. Cabanellas, Guillermo and Luis Bertone. Host Country Taxation of Transfer of Technology Transactions. 11 Ga. J. Int'l & Comp. L. 495 (1981).

1885. Camp, Hope H., Jr. and Carlos Rojas-Magnin. Recent Developments under the Mexican Foreign Investment Law and the Law Regulating the Transfer of Technology. 8 Lawyer of the Americas 1 (1976).

1886. Carl, Beverly May. Technology Transfer: Laws and Practice in Latin America. Chicago: ABA Section on Int'l Law and Practice (1980).

1887. Castilla, Emilio G. de, Jr. Memorandum: New Mexican Law on Transfer of Technology. Reid and Priest, New York, New York, Feb. 2, 1982.

1888. Correa, Carlos M. Transfer of Technology in Latin America: A Decade of Control. 15 J. World Trade L., No. 5 (1981).

1889. Ebb, Lawrence F. Transfer of Foreign Technology in Latin America: The Birth of Antitrust Law? 43 Fordham L. Rev. 719 (1975).

1890. Goytia, Daniel. Technology Transfer in Argentina: First Results under the New Law. 78 Pat. & TM. Rev. 205 (1980).

1891. Hyde, Alan L. & Gastón Ramírez de la Corte. Mexico's 1976 Law of Invention and Trademarks. 12 Case W. Res. J. Int'l L. 469 (1980).

1892. Hyde, Alan L. 1981 Mexican Transfer of Technology Law. 15 Lawyer of the Americas 37 (1983)

1893. Kantor, Newman. D. Restrictions on Technology Transfer in Latin America. 68 Trademark Rep. 552 (1978).

1894. Kryzda, Bill F. Joint Ventures and Technology Transfers (Mexico). 12 Case Western Res. J. Int'l L. 549 (1980).

1895. Mirabito, A. J. Control of Technology Transfer: The Burke-Hartke Legislation and the Andean Foreign Investment Act: The MNE Faces the Nations. 9 Int. Law. 215 (1978).

1896. Nattier, Frank E. Limitations on Marketing Foreign Technology in Brazil. 11 Int'l Lawyer 437 (1977).

1897. Pan American Union, ed. Copyright Protection in the Americas. 3d ed. Rev. Washington (1962, supp. 1967).

1898. Pate, John R. Present and Future Venezuelan Technology Policies: Implementation and Implications for Technology Suppliers and Foreign Investors. 9 Lawyer of the Americas 1 (1977).

1899. Perey, Ron J. and Thomas J. Skola. The Termination of Representation Agreements: The Application of Foreign Law and The Concept of Abuso de Derecho. 11 Calif. Western Int'l L. J. 32 (1981).

1900. Radway, Robert J. Comparative Evolution of Technology Transfer Policies in Latin America: The Practical Realities. 9 Denver J. Int'l L. & Policy 197 (1980).

1901. ________________. Negotiating with Latin American Governments: Technology Transfer and Service Agreements. 9 Lawyer of the Americas 282 (1977).

1902. _____________. Antitrust, Technology Transfers and Joint Ventures in Latin American Developments. 15 Lawyer of the Americas 47 (1983).

1903. Ramírez de la Corte, Gastón and Alan L. Hyde. Mexico's 1976 Law of Inventions and Trademarks. 12 Case Western Res. J. Int'l L. 469 (1980).

1904. ____________. Mexico's New Transfer of Technology and Foreign Investment Laws - To What Extent Have the Rules Changed? 10 Am. J. Int'l L. 231 (1976).

1905. Roffe, P. International Code of Conduct on Transfer of Technology. 11 J. World Trade Law 186 (1977).

1906. Tancer, Robert S. and John P. Zanotti. The Mexican Law of Foreign Real Estate Investment in the Prohibited Zones: An Overview 1971-73. 2d ed. Tempe: Arizona State Univ. Press (1975).

1907. Willis, Neal E. Trademarks in Argentina, Brazil and Andean Pact Countries - A United States Perspective. 66 _Trademark Rep._ 183 (1976).

1908. Wilner, Gabriel M. The Transfer of Technology to Latin America. 14 _Vanderbilt J. Transnat'l L._ 269 (1981).

1909. Wionczek, Miguel S., Gerardo M. Bueno & Jorge E. Navarrete. _La Transferencia Internacional de Tecnología: El Caso de México_. México: Fondo de Cultura Económica (1974).

b. _The Diplomat and Foreign Dignitaries_

1910. Pillado-Salas, Ricardo. The Legal Status of Inter-National Officials. 6 _Inter-Am. L. Rev._ 169 (1964).

1911. Ronning, C. Neale. _Diplomatic Asylum: Legal Norms and Political Reality in Latin American Relations_. The Hague: Nijhoff (1965).

c. _The Visiting Fact-Finder_

1912. Amnesty International. Danish Medical Group. _Evidence of Torture: Studies of the AI Medical Group_. London: Amnesty International Publications (1977).

1913. ________________. _Report of an Amnesty International Mission to Argentina, Nov. 6-15, 1976_. London: Amnesty International Publications (1977).

1914. Bortnick, Jane. International Information Flow: The Developing World Perspective. 14 _Cornell Int'l L. J._ 333 (1981).

1915. Inter-Church Committee on Chile. _One Gigantic Prison: The Report of the Fact-Finding Mission to Chile, Argentina and Uruguay_. Toronto: Inter-Church Committee on Chile (1976).

1916. International Commission of Jurists. _Report on the Situation of Defense Lawyers in Argentina, March, 1975_. Geneva: ICJ (1975).

1917. International League for Human Rights. _Report of a Mission to Argentina, 18-25 January 1978_. New York: The League (1978).

1918. National Academy of Sciences. National Academy of Sciences Committee on Human Rights: Results of a Visit to Argentina and Uruguay. Washington: National Academy of Sciences (1978).

d. The Refugee

1919. Abramovsky, Abraham and Steven J. Eagle. A Critical Evaluation of the Mexican-American Transfer of Penal Sanctions Treaty. 64 Iowa L. Rev. 275 (1979).

1920. Asilo y protección internacional de refugiados en América Latina. México: UNAM (1982).

1921. Mitchell, Glenn H. Aviation: Cuba Withdraws from Anti-Hijack Agreement. 9 Lawyer of the Americas 205 (1977).

1922. Ronning, C. Neale. Diplomatic Asylum. Legal Norms and Political Reality in Latin American Relations. The Hague: Nijhoff (1965).

1923. Schleifer, Nancy. Territorial Asylum in the Americas. 12 Lawyer of the Americas 359 (1980).

1924. Vagts, Detlev. A Reply to "A Critical Evaluation of the Mexican-American Transfer of Penal Sanctions Treaty". 64 Iowa L. Rev. 325 (1979).

1925. Vries, Henry P. de and Jose Rodríguez Novás. Territorial Asylum in the Americas: Latin American Law and Practice of Extradition. 5 Inter. Am. L. Rev. 61 (1963).

e. Other

1926. Beattie, Chester S., Jr. The 1980 Lei Do Estrangiero: The Return of Traditional Defenses Against Expulsion in Brazilian Immigration Laws? 18 Tex. Int'l. L. J. 151 (1983).

1927. Dawson, Frank G. International Law, National Tribunals, and the Rights of Aliens: The Latin American Experience. 21 Vanderbilt L. Rev. 712 (1968).

1928. Garza, E. de la, et al. Should People Stay Home? Regulation of Free Movement and Right of Establishment Between the U.S., Canada and Mexico. 68 Proc. Am Soc'y Int'l L. 38 (1974).

1929. Irizarry y Puente, J. Exclusion and Expulsion of Aliens in Latin America. 36 Am. J. Int'l Law 252 (1942).

1930. Lacey, Frank M. Protection of Foreigners Rights in Mexico. 13 Int'l Lawyer 83 (1979).

1931. Miller, R. Mexican Jails and American Prisoners. 51 Labor J. 439 (1976).

1932. Turack, Daniel C. Freedom of Movement in the Caribbean Community. 11 Denver J. Int'l L. and Policy 37 (1981).

3. Sovereignty and Territoriality

a. Non-Intervention in Domestic Affairs: Latin American Theory and Practice

1933. Blasier, Cole and Carmelo Mesa-Lago, eds. Cuba in the World. Pittsburgh: Univ. of Pittsburgh Press (1979).

1934. Castro, Fidel. Fidel in Chile. Major Speeches During Field Castro's Visit to Chile. New York: International Publishers (1972).

1935. Goldenberg, Boris. The Cuban Revolution and Latin America. New York: Praeger (1965).

1936. Mesa-Lago, Carmel and June S. Belkin, eds. Cuba in Africa. Pittsburgh: University Center for Latin American Studies, Univ. of Pittsburgh (1982).

1937. Taber, Michael, ed. Fidel Castro Speeches: Cuba's Internationalist Foreign Policy 1975-80. New York: Pathfinder Press (1981).

1938. Weinstein, Martin, ed. Revolutionary Cuba in the World Arena. Philadelphia: ISHI (1979).

b. Territorial Disputes and Their Settlement

1) Intra-Continental and Hemispheric Conflicts

1939. Anderson, Thomas P. The War of the Dispossessed: Honduras and El Salvador 1969. Lincoln: Univ. of Nebraska Press (1981)

1940. Barton, Robert. A Short History of the Republic of Bolivia. 2d ed. La Paz: Editorial Los Amigos del Libro. (1968).

1941. Birken, Arthur M. Gulf of Venezuela: Border Dispute. 6 Lawyer of the Americas 52 (1974).

1942. Davis, Harold E., John J. Finan, and F. Taylor Peck. Latin American Diplomatic History: An Introduction. Baton Rouge: Louisiana State Univ. Press (1977).

1943. Dennis, William J. Tacna and Arica: An Account of the Chile-Peru Boundary Dispute and of the Arbitration by the United States. New Haven: Yale Univ. Press (1931).

1944. ___________. Documentary History of the Tacna-Arica Dispute. Iowa City: Univ. of Iowa Press (1927).

1945. Fifer, J. Valerie. Bolivia: Land, Location and Politics Since 1825. Cambridge: Cambridge Univ. Press (1972).

1946. Franck, Thomas M. The Stealing of the Sahara. 70 Am. J. Int'l L. 694 (1976).

1947. Gordon, Michael W., ed. Materials on International Conflicts in the Western Hemisphere, 3d ed. Gainesville: Univ. of Florida (1981).

1948. Himmelreich, David M. The Beagle Channel Affair: A Failure in Judicial Persuasion. 12 Vanderbilt J. Transnat'l L. 971 (1979).

1949. "Honduras: On the Border of War." NACLA Report on the Americas, Vol. 15, No. 6 (Nov.-Dec. 1981).

1950. Ireland, Gordon. Boundaries, Possessions and Conflicts in Central and North America and the Caribbean Cambridge, MA. Harvard University Press (1941).

1951. Millington, Herbert. American Diplomacy and the War of the Pacific. New York: Columbia University Press (1948).

1952. Morris, Michael and Victor Millán, Eds. Controlling Latin American Conflicts: Ten Approaches. Boulder: Westview Press (1983).

1953. Notes and Comment: The Beagle Channel Affair. 71 Am. J. Int'l L. 733 (1977).

1954. Nweihed, Kaldone. "EZ (Uneasy) Delimitation in the Semi-enclosed Caribbean Sea: Recent Agreements between Venezuela and Her Neighbors. 8 Ocean Devel. & Int'l L.J. 1 (1980).

1955. Porras-Barrenechea, Raúl and Alberto Wagner de Reyna. Historia de los Límites del Perú. Lima: Editorial Universitaria (1981).

1956. Rowles, James. El Conflicto Honduras-El Salvador y El Orden Jurídico Internacional (1969). San José: Editorial Universitaria Centroamericana (Costa Rica) (1980).

1957. Wilson, Joe F. The United States, Chile and Peru in the Tacna Arica Plebiscite. Washington: University Press of America (1979).

2) Conflicts with Colonial Powers

1958. Acevedo, Domingo E. The U.S. Measures Against Argentina Resulting from the Malvinas Conflict. 78 Am. J. Int'l L. 323 (1984).

1959. Bianchi William J. Belize: The Controversy Between Guatemala and Great Britain Over the Territory of British Honduras in Central America. New York: Las Americas Publishing Co. (1959).

1960. Bloomfield, Louis M. The British Honduras-Guatemala Dispute. Toronto: Carswell Co. (1953).

1961. Bracey, Audrey. Resolution of the Dominican Crisis, 1965. A study in Mediation. Washington: Georgetown University School of Foreign Service Institute for the Study of Diplomacy (1980).

1962. Caillet-Bois. Ricardo R. Las Islas Malvinas, Una tierra Argentina. Buenos Aires: Ediciones Peuser (1948).

1963. Carril, Bonifacio, del. The Malvinas/Falklands Case. Buenos Aires: Camara de Industriales Graficos de la Argentina (1982).

1964. Davis, Harold E, John J. Finan, F. Taylor Peck. Latin American Diplomatic History: An Introduction. Baton Rouge: Louisiana State University Press (1977)

1965. The Falklands War: The Official History. London: Latin American Newsletters Ltd. (1983).

1966. Freedman, Lawrence. The War of the Falkland Islands, 1982. 61 Foreign Affairs 196 (1982).

1967. Goebel, Julius, Jr. The Struggle for the Falkland Islands: A Study in Legal and Diplomatic History. New Haven: Yale Univ. Press (1982).

1968. Gordon, Michael W., ed. Materials on International Conflicts in the Western Hemisphere. Gainesville: Univ. of Florida 3d ed. (1981).

1969. Hoffmann, Fritz and Olga M. Hoffmann. Sovereignty in Dispute: The Falklands/Malvinas, 1493-1982. Boulder: Westview Press (1984).

1970. Hope, Adrian I.J. Sovereignty and Decolonization of the Malvinas (Falklands) Islands. 6 Boston Coll. Int'l & Comp. L. Rev. 391 (1983).

1971. Immerman, Richard H. The CIA in Guatemala: The Foreign Policy of Intervention. Austin: Univ. of Texas Press (1982).

1972. La Feber, Walter. The Panama Canal: The Crisis in Historical Perspective. Oxford Univ. Press (1978).

1973. Larson, Everette E. A Selective Listing of Monographs and Government Documents on the Falkland/ Malvinas Islands in the Library of Congress. Washington: U.S. Library of Congress, Hispanic Division (1982).

1974. Lavar, M. An Annotated Bibliography of the Falkland Islands. Capetown: Univ. of Capetown (1974).

1975. Lindsey, John M. Conquest: A Legal and Historical Analysis of the Root of United Kingdom Title in the Falkland Islands. 18 Tex. Int'l L. J. 11 (1983).

1976. Loring, David C. The United States-Peruvian "Fisheries" Dispute. 23 Stan. L. Rev. 414 (1971).

1977. Morris, Michael A. and Victor Millan, Eds. Controlli Latin American Conflicts: Ten Approaches. Boulder: Westview Press (1983).

1978. Mummer, Stephen P. The U.S.-Mexican Conflict over Transboundary Groundwaters. 12 Case Western Res. J. Int'l L. 505 (1980).

1979. Muñoz Azpiri, José L. Historia Completa de Las Malvinas. Buenos Aires: Ed. Oriente (1966).

1980. Newfarmer, Richard, ed. From Gunboats to Diplomacy: New U.S. Policies for Latin America. Baltimore: Johns Hopkins Univ. Press (1984).

1981. Pinto, Mónica. Argentina's Rights to the Falklands/Malvinas Islands. 18 Tex. Int'l L. J. 1 (1983).

1982. Report of the President's National Bipartisan Commission on Central America. New York: MacMillan (1984).

1983. Schlesinger, Stephen and Stephen Kinzer. Bitter Fruit: The Untold Story of the American Coup in Guatamala. Garden City: Doubleday (1983).

1984. Tocups, Nora M. City Growth and Cooperation Along the United States/Mexican Border. 10 Ga. J. Int'l & Comp. L. 619 (1980).

1985. Utton, Albert E. International Groundwater Management: The Case of the U.S.-Mexican Frontier. 57 Nebraska L. Rev. 633 (1978).

1986. Wiarda, Howard J. ed. Rift and Revolution: The Central American Imbroglio. Washington: American Enterprise Institute for Public Policy Research (1984).

1987. Wilson, Larman C. The Settlement of Boundary Disputes: Mexico, The United States, and the International Boundary Commission. 29 Int'l & Comp. L. Q. 38 (1980).

4. The Law of the Sea

1988. Carl, Beverly M. Latin American Laws Affecting Coastal Zones. 10 Lawyer of the Americas 51 (1978).

1989. Dickey, Margaret. Should the Law of the Sea Conference be Saved? 12 Int'l Lawyer 1 (1978).

1990. Ferrero Costa, Eduardo. El Nuevo Derecho del Mar: El Peru Y las 200 Milas. Lima: Pontificia Univ. Católica del Perú Fondo Editorial (1979).

1991. Fisher, Joel M., Scott Wood, and Evan T. Burge. Latin American Unilateral Declarations of 200-mile Offshore Exclusive Fisheries: Toward Resolving the Problems of Access Faced by the U.S. Tunafish Industry. 9 Southwestern U. L. Rev. 643 (1977).

1992. Hjertonsson, Karin. The New Law of the Sea: Influence of the Latin American States on Recent Developments of the Law of the Sea. Leiden: Sijthoff (1973).

1993. Leonhard, Alan T. Ixtoc I: A Test for the Emerging Concept of the Patrimonial Sea. 17 San Diego L. Rev 617 (1980).

1994. McClendon, J. Stewart. Some Legal Aspects of Offshore Oil Operations in South America. 1 Inter-Am. L. Rev. 167 (1959).

1995. Morris, Morris. A. Influence and Innovation in the Law of the Sea: Latin America and Africa. 7 Ocean Devel. & Int. L.J. 1 (1979).

1996. Nweihed, Kaldone. G. Venezuela's Contribution to the Contemporary Law of the Sea. 11 San Diego L. Re 603 (1974).

1997. Orrego Vicuña, Francisco. The Regime for the Exploitation of the Seabed Mineral Resources and the Quest for a New International Economic Order of the Oceans: A Latin American View. 10 Lawyer of the Americas 774 (1978).

1998. Pohl, R. Galindo. Latin America's Influence and Role in the Third Conference on the Law of the Sea. 7 Ocean Devel. & Int. L. 65 (1979).

1999. Suman, Daniel. O. A Comparison of the Law of the Sea Claims of Mexico and Brazil. 10 Ocean Devel. & Int. L. J. 131 (1981).

2000. Szekely, Alberto. Latin America and the Development of the Law of the Sea. Regional Documents and National Legislation. Dobbs Ferry: Oceana (1976-1978).

2001. Zacklin, Ralph, ed. The Changing Law of the Sea: Western Hemisphere Perspectives. Leiden: Sijthoff (1974).

## 5. Conflicts of Law and Other "Private" International Law Doctrines

2002. Barnes, William S. Revision of the Bustamante Code. Habana: Academia Interamericana de Derecho Comparad e Internacional (1957).

2003. Bayitch, Stojan A. Inter-American Law of Fisheries. Dobbs Ferry, NY: Oceana (1952).

2004. Bustamante, Antonio S. de. The American Systems on the Conflict of Laws and Their Reconciliation. 5 Tulane L. Rev. 536 (1931).

2005. Gallardo, Ricardo. The Law of Domicile: A Remarkable Connecting Link in Latin American Conflict of Laws. 2 Inter-Am. L. Rev. 61 (1960).

2006. Goldschmidt, Werner and Joan Rodríguez-Novás. American-Argentine Private International Law. Dobbs Ferry: Oceana (1966).

2007. Kuhn, Arthur K. The Scope of Private International Law in Latin American Countries Compared with the Conflict of Laws in the United States. 15 Tulane L. Rev. 394 (1941).

2008. Lazcano, Carlos A. Derecho Internacional Privado. La Plata: Editora Platense (1965).

2009. Nadelmann, Kurt H. Clouds Over International Efforts to Unify Rules of Conflict of Laws. 41 Law & Contemp. Prob. 54 (1977).

2010. ______________. Inter-American Cooperation in the Field of Conflict of Laws. 1 Inter-Am. L. Rev. 135 (1959).

2011. Núñez, E. R. Elementos de Derecho Internacional Privado (1898).

2012. Nussbaum, A., ed. Bilateral Studies in Private International Law. New York: Columbia University, Parker School of Foreign and Comparative Law (1951- ).

2013. Ritch, James E., Jr. Codification of the Private International Law of the American Countries. 7 Inter-Am. L. Rev. 395 (1965).

2014. Siqueiros, José Luis. Private International Law in Mexico and the United States: A Brief Comparative Study. 5 Calif. West. L. Rev. 257 (1970).

2015. Somerville Senn, Hernán. Uniformidad del Derecho Internacional Privado Convencional Americano. Santiago: Editorial Jurídica de Chile (1965).

2016. Zuccherino, R. M. Los Tratados de Montevideo-Analisis Histórico, Comparativo y Crítico. La Plata: Ediciones Librería Jurídica (1973).

6. Participation in International Organizations

a. United Nations

2017. Bossuyt, Marc. The United Nations and Civil and Political Rights in Chile. 27 Int'l and Comp. L. Q. 462 (1978).

2018. Vicente-Moreno, José. Las Naciones Unidas en el Ambito Centroamericano. San Salvador: Min. de Educación (1970).

b. Association of Non-Aligned Nations

2019. Castro, Fidel. We Represent the Immense Majority of Humanity. Speech, UN General Assembly, Oct. 12, 1979. Intercontinental Press/Imprecor (1979).

c. Organization of Petroleum Exporting Countries

2020. Faud. "Venezuela's Role in OPEC: Past, Present & Future", in Robert D. Bond, ed., Contemporary Venezuela and Its Role in International Affairs. New York: New York Univ. Press (1977).

d. Organization of American States

2021. Ball, Mary Margaret. The OAS in Transition. Durham: Duke Univ. Press (1969).

2022. Fenwick, Charles G. The OAS: The Transition From an Unwritten to a Written Constitution. 59 Am. J. Int'l L. 315 (1965).

2023. Fernańdez-Shaw,Felix. La Organización de los Estados Americanos (O.E.A.): Una Nueva Visión de América. 2d ed. Madrid: Ediciones Cultura Hispánica (1963).

2024. Haas, Ernst B. Technological Self-Reliance for Latin America: The OAS Contribution. 34 Int'l Organization 541 (1980).

2025. LeBlanc, Lawrence J. The OAS and the Promotion and Protection of Human Rights. The Hague: Martinus Nijhoff (1977).

2026. Padilla, David J. Administrative Tribunal of the Organization of American States. 44 Lawyer of the Americas 259 (1982)

2027. Thomas, Ann Van Wynen and A.J. Thomas, Jr. The Organization of American States. Dallas: Southern Methodist Univ. Press (1963).

2028. Wood, Bryce. The Organization of American States. 33 Yearbook of World Affairs 148 (1979).

e. COMECON

2029. Clissold, Stephan. Soviet Relations with Latin America, 1918-1968. London: Oxford Univ. Press (1970).

2030. Hewett, Edward A. "Cuba's Membership in the CMEA," in Martin Weinstein, ed., Revolutionary Cuba in the World Arena. Philadelphia: ISHI (1979).

## 7. The Shaping of a Law of Human Rights

a. General

2031. Alarcón, Rodrigo. Brasil: Represión y tortura. Santiago: Editorial Orbe (1971).

2032. Albert, Paul. The Undermining of The Legal Standards for Human Rights Violations in United States Foreign Policy: The Case of "Improvement" in Guatemala. 14 Colum. Human Rts. L. Rev. 231 (1983).

2033. Amnesty International. Report on Torture. (with a Special Report on Chile by Rose Styron). New York: Farrar, Straus and Giroux (1975).

2034. ______________. Chile: Evidence of Torture. London: Amnesty International Publications (1983).

2035. ______________. Testimony on Secret Detention Camps in Argentina. London: Amnesty International Publications (1980).

2036. Armstrong, Robert and Janet Shenk. El Salvador: The Face of Revolution. Boston: South End Press (1982).

2037. Bauer, Carlos G. The Observance of Human Rights and the Structure of the System for Their Protection in the Western Hemisphere. 30 Am. U. L. Rev. 5 (1980).

2038. Berman, Maureen and Roger S. Clark. State Terrorism Disappearances. 13 Rutgers L. J. 531 (1982).

2039. Buergenthal, Thomas, Robert Norris and Dinah Shelton. Protecting Human Rights in the Americas: Selected Problems. Kehl, Strasbourg, Arlington: N.P. Engal (1982).

2040. Camargo, Pedro P. The Right to Judicial Protection: Amparo and Other Latin American Remedies for the Protection of Human Rights. 3 Lawyer of the Americas 191 (1971).

2041. Cassese, Antonio. Foreign Economic Assistance and Respect for Civil and Political Rights: Chile - A Case Study. 14 Tex. Int'l L. J. 251 (1979).

2042. Chomsky, Noam and Edward S. Herman. The Washington Connection and Third World Fascism. Vol. 1, ch. 4. Boston: South End Press (1979).

2043. Cohen, Roberta. Human Rights Diplomacy: The Carter Administration and the Southern Cone. 4 Human Rights Q. 212 (1982).

2044. Comparative Study of the International Covenants on Human Rights Together with the Optional Protocol to the International Covenant on Civil and Political Rights Adopted by the United Nations (December 1966), the Draft Convention on Human Rights of the Inter-American Council of Jurists (Fourth Meeting, 1959) and the Text of the Amendments to the IACJ Draft Adopted by the Inter-America Commission on Human Rights (October 1966 and January 1967). Washington: OAS General Secretariat (1968). (Doc. #OEA/Ser.L/V/11.19 doc. 4).

2045. Crahan, Margaret E., ed. Human Rights and Basic Needs in the Americas. Washington: Georgetown Univ. Press (1982).

2046. Domínguez, Jorge I. The Performance of the Cuban Revolution: A Provisional Assessment. 67 Am. Soc. Int. L. Proc. 205 (1973).

2047. ________________. "An Assessment of Human Rights Conditions", in Human Rights and International Relations, ed. Jorge Domínguez, Richard Falk, Nigel Rodley, and Ben Whitaker. New York: McGraw-Hill (1978).

2048. Draper, Thomas, ed. Democracy and Dictatorship in Latin America. New York: H. W. Wilson (1981).

2049. Duff, Ernest A. and John F. McCamant. Violence and Repression in Latin America: A Quantitative and Historical Analysis. New York: Free Press (1976).

2050. El Salvador: Background to the Crisis. Cambridge: Central America Information Office (1982).

2051. Faculty for Human Rights in El Salvador and Central America. Education and Human Rights in El Salvador. Report, National Faculty Delegation to El Salvador, January 3-10, 1983. Berkeley: Univ. of Cal. (1983).

2052. Farer, Tom J. Human Rights and Human Welfare in Latin America. 112 Daedalus No. 4 (Fall 1983), p.139.

2053. Ferguson, Clarence Clyde, Jr. Economic Development and Human Rights: Brazil, Chile and Cuba: A Panel. 67 Am. Soc. Int. L. Proc. 198 (1973).

2054. Fisher, Stewart W. Human Rights in El Salvador and U.S. Foreign Policy. 4 Human Rights Q. 1 (1982).

2055. Fox, Donald T. Doctrinal Development in the Americas: From Non-Intervention to Collective Support for Human Rights. 1 N.Y.U. J. Int'l L. & Pol. 44 (1968).

2056. Fruhling, Hugo. Stages of Repression and Legal Strategy for the Defense of Human Rights in Chile: 1973-1980. 5 Human Rights Q. 510 (1983).

2057. Gallón Giraldo, Gustavo. Quince años de estado de sitio en Colombia, 1958-1978. Bogotá: Librería y Editorial América Latina (1979).

2058. Goldman, Robert K. The Protection of Human Rights in the Americas: Past, Present and Future. New York: NYU Center for International Studies (1972).

2059. Greenfield, Richard. The Human Rights Literature of Latin America. 4 Human Rights Quarterly 275 (1982).

2060. Hennelly, Alfred, S.J., and John Langan, S.J., eds. Human Rights in the Americas: The Struggle for Consensus. Washington: Georgetown Univ. Press (1982).

2061. Human Rights in the American States: A Study Prepared in Accordance with Resolution XXVII of the Tenth Inter-American Conference. Prelim. ED. Pan American Union Codification Division, ed. Washington: OAS General Secretariat (1960).

2062. Human Rights in Guatemala. Hearing, Subcom. on Human Rights and International Organizations and Subcom. on Inter-American Affairs, Comm. on Foreign Affairs, U.S. House of Representatives, 97th Cong. 1st sess., July 30, 1981.

2063. Inter-American Commission on Human Rights. Report on the Situation of Human Rights in Argentina. Washington, D.C.: General Secretariat, Organization of American States (1980).

2064. Inter-Church Committee on Chile. One Gigantic Prison: The Report of the Fact-Finding Mission to Chile, Argentina and Uruguay. Toronto: Inter-Church Committee on Chile (1976).

2065. International League of Human Rights ("ILHR"). Mbareté: The Higher Law of Paraguay. Report on the Denial of Human Rights in Paraguay by the Third Commission of Enquiry of the International League for Human Rights. New York: ILHR (May, 1980).

2066. ______________. Mbareté: Two Years Later. New York: ILHR (June, 1982).

2067. Jonas, Susanne and David Tobis, Eds. Guatemala. New York: North American Council on Latin America (1974).

2068. Kass, Stephen L. and Juan E. Mendy. On Human Rights in Nicaragua: An Americas Watch Report. New York: Americas Watch (1982).

2069. Latin American Newsletter, Ltd. Torture in Latin America. 10 Latin America No. 12 (March 19, 1976), p. 91.

2070. LeBlanc, Lawrence J. Economic, Social and Cultural Rights and the Inter American System. 19 J. Inter-Am. Studies and World Affairs 61 (Feb. 1977).

2071. Lernoux, Penny. Cry of the People: The Struggle for Human Rights in Latin America - The Catholic Church in Conflict With U.S. Policy. New York: Penguin (1982).

2072. Maechling, Charles, Jr. The Argentine Pariah. Foreign Policy, Winter 1981/1982, p. 69.

2073. Marmorstein, Victoria E. World Bank Power to Consider Human Rights Factors in Loan Decisions. 13 J. Int'l L. & Econ. 113 (1978).

2074. Montealegre, Hernan. Human Rights in the History and Culture of Latin America. San Jose: Instituto Interamericano de Derechos Humanos. Feb 14, 1983.

2075. Murray, Daniel E. A Comparative Study of Peruvian Criminal Procedure. 21 Univ. Miami L. Rev. 607 (1967).

2076. __________. Seguridad del Estado y los Derechos Humanos. Santiago: Academia de Humanismo Cristiano (1979).

2077. Nash, Richard, Jr. Certifying Human Rights: Military Assistance to El Salvador and The International Security and Development Cooperation Act of 1981. 14 Colum. Human Rts. L. Rev. 275 (1983).

2078. Organization of American States and Human Rights, 1960-1967. Washington: OAS General Secretariat (1972).

2079. Organization of American States, Inter-American Commission on Human Rights. Fifth Report on the States of Human Rights in Cuba. OEA/Ser. G/CP/INF. 872/76, June 1, 1976. Washington, D.C.: OAS General Secretariat (1976).

2080. ______________. Report Regarding the Situation of Human Rights in Cuba. OEA/Ser. L/V/II. 17, Doc. 4 rev., June 13, 1967. Washington, D.C.: OAS General Secretariat (1967).

2081. Posner, Michael H. and R. Scott Greathead. Justice in El Salvador: A Report by the Lawyers Committee for International Human Rights on the Investigation into the Killing of Four U.S. Church Women. 14 Colum. Human Rts. L. Rev. 191 (1983).

2082. Review of United States Policy on Military Assistance to Argentina. Joint Hearing Before Subcomm. on Human Rights and Int'l Organizations and Subcomm. on Inter-American Affairs, Comm. on Foreign Affairs, U.S. House of Representatives, 97th Cong., 1st Sess. April 1, 1981.

2083. Report on the Situation of Human Rights in the Republic of Bolivia. Inter-American Commission on Human Rights, ed. Washington: Organization of American States. (1981).

2084. Report on the Situation of Human Rights in the Republic of Colombia. Inter-American Commission on Human Rights, ed. Washington: Organization of American States. (1981).

2085. Report on the Situation of Human Rights in the Republic of Guatemala. Washington: General Secretariat, Organization of American States. (1981).

2086. Report on the Situation of Human Rights in the Republic of Nicaragua. Inter-American Commission on Human Rights, ed. Washington: Organization of American States. (1981).

2087. Rojas, Fernando. El Estado en los ochenta: hacia un régimen político. Bogotá: Centro de Investigació y Educación Popular (1980).

2088. Role of Nongovernmental Organizations in Implementing Human Rights in Latin America. 7 Ga. J. Int'l & Comp. L. 477 (1977).

2089. Ronning, C. Neale. Human Rights and Humanitarian Laws in the Western Hemisphere. 38 Soc. Res. 320 (1971).

2090. Rotman, Edgardo. La Protection des Droits de l'Homme en Matiere Peńale dans le Droit Argentin et Latino - Americain. 47 Revue Internationale de Droit Penal 83 (Sept. 1979).

2091. Russell Tribunal II on Repression in Brazil, Chile and Latin America. Found Guilty: The Verdict of the Russell Tribunal Session in Brussels. Spokesman Pamphlet No. 51. Nottingham: Bertrand Russell Peace Foundation for the Spokesman (1976).

2092. ______________, 1st sess., Rome, 1974. Repression in Latin America: A Report on the First Session of the Second Russell Tribunal, Rome, April 1974. Ed. & Trans. William Jerman. Nottingham: Bertrand Russell Peace Foundation for Spokesman Books (1975).

2093. Schoutz, Lars. Human Rights and United States Policy toward Latin America. Princeton: Princeton U. Press (1981).

2094. The Situation of Human Rights in Cuba. Seventh Report. Inter-American Commission on Human Rights, ed. Washington: Organization of American States (1983).

2095. Sohn, Louis B. Torture as a Violation of the Law of Nations. 11 Ga.J. Int'l Comp. L. 307 (1981).

2096. Timerman, Jacobo. Prisoner Without a Name, Cell Without a Number. Trans. Tony Talbot. New York: Knopf (distributed by Random House) (1981).

2097. Turack, Daniel C. Freedom of Movement in the Caribbean Community. 11 Denver Journal of Int'l Law and Policy 37 (1981).

2098. Turner, John Kenneth. Barbarous Mexico. Austin: University of Texas Press (1969).

2099. Tyson, Beverly. Economic Growth and Human Rights in Brazil. 67 Am. Soc. Int. L. Proc. 208 (1973).

2100. Wiarda, Howard J., et al. eds. Human Rights and United States Human Rights Policy: Theoretical Approaches and Some Perspectives on Latin America. Washington: American Enterprise Institute for Public Policy Research (1982).

2101. Wilner, Gabriel M. Filartiga v. Pena-Irala: Comments on Sources of Human Rights Law and Means of Redress for Violations of Human Rights. 11 Ga. J. Int'l & Comp. L. 317 (1981).

b. The Inter-American Convention

2102. Anotación sobre el Proyecto de Convención Inter-americana sobre Protección de Derechos Humanos. Washington: OAS General Secretariat (1969). Doc. # OEA/Ser. L/V/11.19 doc. 53.

2103. Buergenthal, Thomas. The American and European Conventions on Human Rights: Similarities and Differences. 30 American U. L. Rev. 155 (1981).

2104. _________, and Robert E. Norris, eds. Human Rights: The Inter-American System. Part 1: Basic Documents. Dobbs Ferry: Oceana (1982).

2105. Handbook of Existing Rules Pertaining to Human Rights. Updated to July 1980. Washington: OAS General Secretariat (1980). (Doc. #OEA/Ser. L/V/11.50 doc. 6.)

2106. Le Blanc, Lawrence J. The Inter-American Commission on Human Rights. 9 Revue des Droits de l' Homme 645 (1976).

2107. Lockwood, Bert B., Jr. The Model American Convention on the Prevention and Punishment of Certain Serious Forms of Violence Jeopardizing Fundamental Rights and Freedoms. 13 Rutgers L. J. 579 (1982).

2108. Monroy-Cabra, Marco G. Rights and Duties Established by the American Convention on Human Rights. 30 American U. L. Rev. 21 (1980).

2109. Norris, Robert E. Bringing Human Rights Petitions Before the Inter-American Commission. 20 Santa Clara L. Rev. 733 (1980).

2110. ________________. The New Statute of the Inter-American Commission on Human Rights. 1 Hum. Rts. J. 379 (1980).

2111. ____________________. Observations in Loco: Practice and Procedure of the Inter-American Commission on Human Rights. 15 Texas Int'l L. J. 46 (1980).

2112. __________. Observations in Loco: Practice and Procedure of the Inter-American Commission on Human Rights, 1979-1983. 19 Tex. Int'l L.J. 284 (1984).

2113. _______________, and Paula D. Reiton. The Suspension of Guarantees: A Comparative Analysis of the American Convention on Human Rights and the Constitutions of the States Parties. 30 Am. U. L. Rev. 189 (1980).

2114. Peddicord, Jane A. The American Convention on Human Rights: Potential Defects and Remedies. 19 Tex. J. Int'l L. 139 (1984).

2115. Schreiber, Anna P. The Inter-American Commission on Human Rights. Leyden: Sijthoff (1970).

2116. Symposium. The American Convention on Human Rights. 30 American U. L. Rev. 1 (1980).

2117. Uribe-Vargas, Diego. Los Derechos Humanos y el Sistema Interamericano (1972).

2118. Volio, Fernando. The Inter-American Commission on Human Rights. 30 American U. L. Rev. 65 (1980).

c. The Inter-American Court of Human Rights

2119. Buergenthal, Thomas. The Inter-American Court of Human Rights. 76 Am. J. Int'l L. 231 (1982).

2120. Castro-Ramírez, Manuel. Cinco Años en la Corte de Justicia Centroamericana, San José: Imp. Lehmann (1918).

2121. Dunshee de Abranches, Carlos A. The Inter-American Court of Human Rights. 30 American U. L. Rev. 79 (1980).

2122. Gutiérrez-Gutiérrez, Carlos José, La Corte de Justicia Centroamericana. San José: Ed. Juricentro (1978).

2123. Martínez Moreno, Alfredo. La Conferencia de Washington de 1907 y La Corte de Justicia Centroamericana. San Salvador: Publicaciones del Ministerio de Relaciones Exteriores (1957).

2124. Vargas-Carreño, Edmundo. Some Problems presented by the Application and Interpretation of the American Convention on Human Rights. 30 American U. L. Rev. 127 (1980).

2125. Ventura, Manuel E. Costa Rica and The Inter. American Court of Human Rights. 4 Human Rights L. J. 273 (1983).

D. Success and Failure in Latin American Regional Integration Movements

2126. Atchabahian, Adolfo, et al. Fiscal Harmonization in the Andean Countries. International Bureau of Fiscal Documentation (1975).

2127. Barnes, William S. Legal Issues in Inter-American Relations. 11 Texas Int'l L. J. 63 (1976).

2128. Bond, Robert D. Regionalism in Latin America: Prospects for the Latin American Economic System (SELA). 32 Int'l Organization 401 (1978).

2129. Connell-Smith, Gordon. The Inter-American System. London: Oxford U. Press (1966).

2130. García Amador y Rodriguez, Francisco Victor. The Andean Legal Order: A New Community Law. Dobbs Ferry: Oceana (1978).

2131. Golbert, Albert S. Customs Union Theory v. Practice 4 Southwestern U. L. Rev. 250 (1972).

2132. ____________, and Yenny Nun. Latin American Economic Integration: An Overview of Trade and Investment Developments in ANCOM, CACM & LAFTA. 7 Syracuse J. Int'l & Comp. L. 183 (1979-1980).

2133. Goldman, Marvin G. Arbitration in Inter-American Trade Relations: Regional Market Aspects. 7 Inter-Am. L. Rev. 67 (1965).

2134. Grunwald, Joseph, Martin Cornay and Miguel S. Wionczek. Latin American Economic Integration and U.S. Policy. Washington D.C. Brookings Institution (1972).

2135. Hemispheric Cooperation of Integral Development: Report for the General Secretariat of the OAS. Washington, D.C.: CIES, General Secretariat of Organization of American States (1982).

2136. Inter-American Institute of International Legal Studies. Instruments of Economic Integration in Latin American and the Caribbean. Dobbs Ferry: Oceana (1975).

2137. ______________. The Inter-American System - Its Development and Strengthening. Dobbs Ferry: Oceana (1966).

2138. Instituto para la Integración de América Latina (INTAL). Los estudios de Derecho Comparado y la multinacionalidad de las empresas en América Latina. 5 Derecho de la Integración 5 (1969).

2139. Maritano, Nino. and Antonio H. Obaid. An Alliance for Progress: The Challenge and the Problem. Minneapolis: Denison (1963).

2140. Onís, Juan de and Jerome Levinson. The Alliance that Lost Its Way: A Critical Report on The Alliance for Progress. Chicago: Quadrangle Books (1970).

2141. Operating in Latin America's Integrating Markets: ANCOM, CACM, CARICOM, LAFTA. New York: Business Int'l Corp. (1977).

2142. Padilla, David J. The Judicial Resolution of Legal Disputes in the Integration Movements of the Hemisphere. 11 Lawyer of the Americas 75 (1979).

2143. Pierson, Samuel B. The Five Inter-American Conventions: In Support of Their Ratification. 9 Lawyer of the Americas 509 (1977).

2144. Ratliff, William. United States Policy Toward the Caribbean. 17 Willamette L. Rev. 221 (1980).

2145. Riesenfeld, Stefan A. Legal Systems of Regional Economic Integration. 22 Am. J. Comp. L. 415 (1974).

2146. Vargas-Hidalgo, Rafael. The Process of Integration in Latin America. 15 Comparative Juridical Rev. 105 (1978).

2147. ______________________. Economic Integration, Development Planning and Sovereignty: A Latin American View. 9 Lawyer of the Americas 318 (1977).

2148. Whitaker, Arthur P. The Western Hemisphere Idea: Its Rise and Decline. Ithaca: Cornell Univ. Press (1954).

2149. Wilner, Gabriel M. and Michael A. & Robinson. Colloquium on Certain Legal Aspects of Inter-American Cooperation: Establishment of the Mechanisms for the Settlement of Economic Disputes; Views in the Americas on Basic Questions Relating to the Law of the Sea. 5 Ga. J. Int'l & Comp. L. 141 (1975).

2150. Wionczek, Miguel S. The Rise and the Decline of Latin American Economic Integration. 9 J. Common Mkt. Studies 49 (1970).

2151. _____________, ed. Integración de América Latina. México: Fondo De Cultura Económica (1964).

1. Latin American Free Trade Association (LAFTA)

2152. Holland, Susan S. and Esteban A. Ferrer. Changing Legal Environment in Latin America: Management Implications. New York: Council of the Americas (1975-1979).

2153. Lee, H. LAFTA Today. 44 Mexican-American Review 24 (1976).

2154. New Integration Treaty Revises Ground Rules and Dismantles LAFTA. Business Latin America 217 (July 9, 1980).

## 2. Andean Pact


2155. Abbott, Frederick M. Bargaining Power and Strategy in the Foreign Investment Process: A Current Andean Code Analysis. 3 Syracuse J. Int'l L. & Com. 319 (1975).

2156. The Andean Foreign Investment Code: An Overview. 7 Georgia J. Int'l & Comp. L. 656 (1977).

2157. Avery, William P. Subregional Integration in Latin America: The Andean Common Market. 11 J. Common Mkt. Studies 85 (1972-73).

2158. Carl, Beverly M., and Lawrence Johnson. Venezuela and the Andean Common Market. 7 Denver J. Int'l L. Pol. 151 (1978).

2159. Carnoy, Martin. Industrialization in Latin American Common Market. Washington, D.C.: Brookings Institution (1972).

2160. Comment: The Colombian Supreme Court Decision on the Andean Foreign Investment Code and Its Implications for the Law of Treaties. 8 J. Int'l L. & Econ. 113 (1973).

2161. Comment. Chile's Rejection of the Andean Common Market Regulation of Foreign Investment. 16 Colum. J. Transnat'l L. 138 (1977).

2162. Council of the Americas. The Andean Pact: Definition, Design, and Analysis. New York: Council of the Americas (1973).

2163. Danino, Roberto. The Andean Code after Five Years. 8 Lawyer of the Americas 635 (1976).

2164. Fouts, Susan C. The Andean Foreign Investment Code. 10 Texas Int'l L. J. 537 (1975).

2165. García Amador y Rodriguez, Francisco Victor. The Andean Legal Order: A New Community Law. Dobbs Ferry: Oceana (1978).

2166. Horton, Scott. Peru and ANCOM: A Study in the Disintegration of a Common Market. 17 Texas Int'l L. J. 39 (1982).

2167. Lisocki, Stanley R. The Andean Investment Code. 49 Notre Dame Lawyer 319 (1973).

2168. Lochridge, Edwin P. The Role of the Andean Court in Consolidating Regional Integration Efforts. 10 Georgia J. Int'l & Comp. L. 351 (1980).

2169. López-Valdéz, Abelardo. The Andean Foreign Investment Code: An Analysis. 7 J. Int'l L. & Econ. 1 (1972).

2170. Morawetz, David. The Andean Group: A Case Study in Economic Integration Among Developing Countries. Cambridge, MA: MIT Press (1974).

2171. The Multinational Enterprise in the Context of Latin American Economic Integration: The Andean Agreement Model. 11 San Diego L. Rev. 245 (1973).

2172. Murphy, Ewel L. E., Jr. The Andean Common Market and Mexico: A Foreign Investment Profile. 13 Texas Int'l L. J. 307 (1978).

2173. Note. Political Components and Practical Effects of the Andean Foreign Investment Code. 27 Stan. L. Rev. 1597 (1975).

2174. Oliver, Covey T. The Andean Foreign Investment Code: A New Phase in the Quest for Normative Order as to Direct Foreign Investment. 66 Am. J. Int'l L. 763 (1972).

2175. Perenzin, Dominic. A. Regulation of the Andean Investment Code: Colombia. 4 Lawyer of the Americas 15 (1972).

2176. Schill, Charles F. The Mexican and Andean Investment Codes: An Overview and Comparison. 6 Law & Policy Int'l Bus. 437 (1974).

2177. Schliesser, Peter, ed. Recent Developments in Latin American Foreign Investment Laws. 6 Int'l Lawyer 64 (1972).

2178. Schydlowsky, Daniel M. Allocating Integration Industries in the Andean Group. 9 J. Common Mkt. Studies 299 (1970-1971).

2179. Stebbings, Robert Y. Argentine Foreign Investment Law and its Andean Common Market Inspiration. 8 Vanderbilt J. Transnat'l L. 277 (1975).

2180. Swan, Alan C. The Andean Code: A Preliminary Appraisal. 5 Lawyer of the Americas 259 (1973).

2181. Vargas-Hidalgo, Rafael. An Evaluation of the Andean Pact. 10 Lawyer of the Americas 401 (1978).

2182. Zamora, Antonio R. Andean Common Market: Regulation of Foreign Investments: Blueprint for the Future. 10 Int'l Lawyer 153 (1976).

3. Central American Common Market

2183. Cline, William R. and Enrique Delgado, eds. Economic Integration in Central America: A Study. Washingto Brookings Institution (1978).

2184. Ereli, Eleizer. The Central American Common Market: Integration in Practice. 43 Tulane L. Rev. 1 (1968).

2185. Gordon, Michael W. Developed, Developing and Dependent Nations: Central American Development in a New Economic Realignment. 11 J. Int'l L. & Eco 1 (1976).

2186. Lizano, Eduardo and L.N. Willmore. Second Thoughts on Central America: The Rosenthal Report. 13 J. Common Mkt. Studies 280 (1975).

2187. Schmitter, Philippe C. Central American Integration: Spill-Over, Spill-Around or Encapsulation? 9 J. Common Mkt. Studies 1 (1970).

2188. Wallace, M., ed. Multinational Corporations Law: Mexico, Central America, Panama and the Central American Common Market. Dobbs Ferry: Oceana (1981).

2189. Watkin, Virginia G. Taxes and Tax Harmonization in Central America. Cambridge, MA.: Law School of Harvard University (1967).

4. Latin America Economic System (SELA)

2190. Bond, Robert D. Regionalism in Latin America: Prospects for the Latin American Economic System (SELA). 32 Int'l Organization 401 (1978).

5. Caribbean Economic Community (CARICOM).

2191. Abbot, Richard L. The Caribbean Free Trade Association. 1 Lawyer of the Americas 1 (1969).

2192. Axline, W. Andrew. Integration and Development in the Commonwealth Caribbean: The Politics of Regional Negotiations. 32 Int'l Organization 953 (1978).

2193. Chernick, Sidney E. The Commonwealth Caribbean: The Integration Experience. Report of a Mission Sent to the Commonwealth Caribbean by the World Bank. Baltimore: Johns Hopkins Univ. Press (1978).

2194. O'Connell, Joseph F., III. The Caribbean Community: Economic Integration in the Commonwealth Caribbean. 11 J. Int'l L. Econ. 35 (1976).

2195. Simmonds, K.R. The Caribbean Economic Community: A New Venture in Regional Integration. 23 Int'l L. Comp. L. Q. 453 (1974).

6. Other

2196. Adams, Mark S. and Barry Steiner. Energy and the North American Community: Canada, Mexico, and the United States. 3 Hastings Int'l & Comp. L. Rev. 369 (1980).

2197. Broderick, Margaret. Associated Statehood - A New Form of Decolonisation. 17 Int'l & Comp. L. Q. 368 (1968).

2198. Comment: Amazon Treaty: A Turning Point in Latin American Cooperation? 15 Tex. Int. L. J. 117 (1980).

2199. Geiser, Hans, Pamela Alleyne and Carroll Gajraj. Legal Problems of Caribbean Integration: A Study on the Legal Aspects of Caricom. Leyden: Sijthoff (1976).

2200. Gilmore, William C. Legal Perspectives on Associated Statehood in the Eastern Caribbean. 19 Virginia J. Int'l L. 489 (1979).

2201. Hill, Humphrey M. Central American Court of Justice. 1 Encyclopedia of Public International Law 41, ed. Rudolf Bernhardt (New York: North-Holland Pub. Co. 1981).

2202. Joyner, Christopher C. Latin America's Communal Response to the Energy Crisis: The Latin American Energy Organization (OLADE). 6 Lawyer of the Americas 637 (1974).

2203. Landau, Georges D. The Treaty for Amazonian Cooperation: A Bold New Instrument for Development. 10 Ga. J. Int'l & Comp. L. 463 (1980).

2204. Lowenthal, Abraham F. Caribbean Basis Initiative: Misplaced Emphasis. Foreign Policy, Summer 1982, p. 114.

2205. Monroy-Cabra, Marco G. Rights and Duties Established by the American Convention on Human Rights. 30 Am. U. L. Rev. 21 (1980).

2206. Mordecai, Sir John. *The West Indies: The Federal Negotiations*. Evanston: London: Allen and Unwin (1968).

2207. Wooding, Sir Hugh. The Failure of the West Indies Federation. 5 *Melbourne U. L. Rev.* 257 (1966).

## E. Northward Migrations: Legal Aspects of Efforts to "Recolonize" Lost Territories

2208. Bettwy, Samuel W. Mexican Transmigration: A Case for the Application of International Law. 10 *Calif. Western Int'l L. J.* 92 (1980).

2209. The Caribbean Exodus. 11 *Caribbean Review* No. 1 (Winter 1982).

2210. Cornelius, Wayne A. Mexican Migration to the United States: The View from Rural Sending Communities. Paper, Conference on Mexico and the United States: The Next Ten Years. School of Int'l Service, American University, Washington, D.C., March 18-19 (1976).

2211. ________, et al. *Mexican Immigrants and Southern California: A Summary of Current Knowledg*[…] San Diego: Univ. of Calif. Center for U.S.-Mexican Studies (1982).

2212. Ehrlich, Paul R., Loy Bilderback, Anne H. Ehrlich. *The Golden Door: International Migration, Mexico, and the United States*. New York: Ballantine Books (1979).

2213. Foster, James C., Ed. *American Labor in the Southwest: The First One Hundred Years*. Tucson: Univ. of Arizona Press (1982).

2214. Gandara, A. *The Chicano/Illegal Alien Civil Liberties Interface*. (Rand Corporation, November 1977).

2215. Gordon, Michael W., ed. *Materials on International Conflicts in the Western Hemisphere*. 3d ed. Gainesville: Univ. of Florida (1981).

2216. López-Valdéz, A., et al. Labor Mobility: The Global Bracero Problem. 73 *Am. Soc'y Int'l L. Proc.* 119 (1979).

2217. Ríos-Bustamante, Antonio. *Mexican Immigrant Workers in the U.S.* Berkeley: UCLA Chicano Studies (1981).

2218. Ronfeldt, D.F. and C.D. Sereseres. Treating the Alien(ation) in U.S.-Mexico Relations. (Rand Corporation, August 1978).

2219. Tocups, Nora M. City Growth and Cooperation along the United States Mexican Border. 10 Ga. J. Int'l & Comp. L. 619 (1980).

2220. Vila, Adis M. Legal Aspects of Foreign Direct Investments in the United States 16 Int'l Lawyer 1 (1982).

2221. Ziskind, David and Esther Horney. Laws Affecting Migratory Labor: United States, Mexico, and Canada. 4 Comp. Labor L. 1 (1981).

## *AUTHOR INDEX*

Numbers below refer to entry, not page, numbers.

**About the Author**

FREDERICK E. SNYDER is Assistant Dean for International and Comparative Legal Studies and a Lecturer on Latin American Law at Harvard Law School. His articles have appeared in *Lawyer of the Americas*, *Journal of Dispute Resolution*, and other scholarly and professional publications.

www.ingramcontent.com/pod-product-compliance
Ingram Content Group UK Ltd.
Pitfield, Milton Keynes, MK11 3LW, UK
UKHW020210290926
15470UKWH00001B/99

9 780313 248580